Mike Bingham is a columnist and feature writer with the Hobart *Mercury*, which he joined in 1979. Before that he had worked for the *Courier Mail* in Brisbane, the *Sydney Morning Herald*, the *Sun* in Melbourne, and as a foreign correspondent for the *Herald & Weekly Times* in London. *Suddenly One Sunday* is his fourth book.

SUDDENLY
ONE SUNDAY

MIKE BINGHAM

HarperCollinsPublishers

HarperCollins_Publishers_

First published in Australia in 1996
by HarperCollins_Publishers_ Pty Limited
ACN 009 913 517
A member of the HarperCollins_Publishers_ (Australia) Pty Limited Group

Copyright © Davies Brothers Ltd 1996

This book is copyright.
Apart from any fair dealing for the purposes of private study, research,
criticism or review, as permitted under the Copyright Act, no part may
be reproduced by any process without written permission.
should be addressed to the publishers.

HarperCollins_Publishers_
25 Ryde Road, Pymble, Sydney NSW 2073, Australia
31 View Road, Glenfield, Auckland 10, New Zealand
77–85 Fulham Palace Road, London W6 8JB, United Kingdom
Hazelton Lanes, 55 Avenue Road, Suite 2900, Toronto, Ontario M5R 3L2
and 1995 Markham Road, Scarborough, Ontario M1B 5M8, Canada
10 East 53rd Street, New York NY 10032, USA

National Library of Australia Cataloguing-in-Publication data:

Bingham, Mike, 1941– .
Suddenly one Sunday.
ISBN 0 7322 5788 3
1. Bryant, Martin. 2. Mass murder – Tasmania – Port Arthur. I. Title.
364.1523

Typeset in 10.5 on 16 point Baskerville

Printed in Australia by Griffin Paperbacks, Netley, South Australia

9 8 7 6 5 4 3 2 1
99 98 97 96

ACKNOWLEDGMENTS

This book exists because the people of Tasmania, particularly those on the Tasman Peninsula, believed it was important that an accurate and sensitive account be written about the events of that terrible day, 28 April 1996. It is not just the record of one man's awful crime, but of the courage and humanity displayed by so many others.

I am grateful for the generous co-operation I have received from the emergency services and from individuals, and hope that this book in some way repays the trust they placed in me.

Thanks also to my Hobart *Mercury* colleagues Janet Weaving, Leigh Winburn, Stuart Potter and Rae Walsh, and to Maggie O'Neill and Prue Purser for the long days and nights they spent transcribing taped interviews. I am also indebted to Jude McGee of HarperCollins, and to my wife, Liz, whose encouragement and constructive criticism were invaluable.

Dedicated to all those who lost their lives at Port Arthur

CONTENTS

Acknowledgments 5
1 One Fine Cool Day 11

PART I THE SHADOW 19
2 The Firecracker Boy 21
3 The Heiress's Heir 28
4 On the Road to Port Arthur 35
5 A Separate World 42
6 The Frequent Flier 48
7 "I'll Think of Something..." 53

PART II BLACK SUNDAY 57
8 Something Wrong at the Seascape Guest House 59
9 A Day for Settling "Scores" 63
10 "Everyone Thought it was a Re-enactment..." 70
11 The Broad Arrow Cafe 73
12 Like Rabbits in a Trap 79
13 Murder on the Road 83
14 A Deathly Quiet 87
15 Operation Code Brown 93
16 A Man Called "Jamie" 97
17 The Negotiator 104
18 Military Tactics 117
19 Innocence Lost 123

PART III A NATION IN SHOCK 127
20 At the Royal Hobart Hospital 129
21 A Sorrow Never Known 135
22 Daffodils Will Bloom 140
23 The Port Arthur Taskforce 154
24 As a Guest of Risdon Prison 165
25 The Trial of Martin Bryant 168

CHAPTER 1

One Fine Cool Day . . .

Sunday was their last day in Tasmania, and they were determined to fit in some sightseeing before flying home to Western Australia. For Mick Sargent, thirty, and his girlfriend, Kate Scott, twenty-one, it had been a lightning visit. The day before, they watched as Mick's friend from Perth Darryl Carter, and his fiancee, Bronwyn, tied the knot at Saint Mary's cathedral in Hobart. Mick had been best man at the wedding.

But time was tight: Mick and Kate were booked to fly from Hobart to Melbourne at 4.15 p.m., to link up with a direct flight home to Perth that night. And that wasn't the end of the marathon: Mick worked in a mine three and a half hours drive from the Western Australian capital, and was due back at work on Monday morning.

The entire trip had been a rush because neither of them had much holiday leave owing. Most of it they had used following the motorcycle drag-racing circuit in Western Australia and interstate.

It was drag racing that had brought them together, three years before, when Mick had spotted Kate at a raceway near Mandurah, 150 kilometres south of Perth. "Kate Scott, VIP" said the badge on her shirt. Mick was planning to start competing in the drag races himself. She must be important, he thought. It might be handy to get to know her.

Back at work at the mine, and determined to test himself in competitive drag racing, Mick had mentally scrolled through a list of female acquaintances, trying to think of someone who could become his "reverse gear". Drag racing is a team effort: you need a driver, a mechanic, and a pretty girl to push the bike back to the start line after the initial "burn-out", which is used to heat up the tyres. The girls were known as reverse gears. But who would be mad enough to do it? He couldn't think of anyone. Then it clicked: "Kate Scott, VIP".

Phoning the racetrack, he spoke to Kate's girlfriend, who worked in the control tower, and convinced her to give him Kate's phone number. He rang it and, after a few preliminaries, announced he was chasing a crew. Would she like to be part of the team: the reverse gear for the next season? Obviously she knew the drill; after all, she was a "VIP".

"You've got to be kidding!" she said. "No way!"

It turned out that Kate had been a casual spectator that day at the racetrack, and the badge had been a gift from her girlfriend. But Mick persevered and Kate finally agreed, on the condition that they meet to talk about it.

Mick and Kate had dinner together in Perth a week or

two later. Kate agreed to help the team. "At least until someone else can do it."

But she grew to love the sport, and became virtual manager of the team, doing the books and accompanying Mick to meetings as far away as New South Wales. In November 1995, they made the quarter finals in Victoria, and Mick broke a couple of Australian records.

Their own relationship was also a winner. Mick was very happy with Kate, and she was very happy with him, and they wanted to spend the rest of their lives together. Kate was keen to marry, and they talked about it a lot. They decided to wait until the following February to become engaged, planning to marry before the start of the new drag-racing season.

When his old mate Darryl announced he was getting married in Hobart and asked him to be best man, Mick immediately agreed, even though money and time were tight. They would both go. Kate's family helped out by paying for her fare.

It had been a wonderful few days in Tasmania, despite the rush, and the wedding was lovely. After the reception Mick and Kate had adjourned to the casino to dance at the disco and have a couple of drinks.

And now it was their last day. At about 10.30 a.m. they heard the sound of a car pulling up outside the holiday cabin they had checked into on the city's eastern shore. It was their friends John Riviere and Caroline Villiers, who had also come to Hobart for the wedding. The foursome had arranged a day of sightseeing. Packed and ready to go, they set off for the famous convict ruins at Port Arthur, an easy ninety-minute drive south-east from Hobart, on the Tasman

Peninsula. The plan was to spend a few hours looking around before dropping off Mick and Kate at Hobart airport to catch their 4.15 flight.

John and Caroline were not in such a rush: they lived in Melbourne, which was only a one-hour hop back across Bass Strait, and their plane wasn't due to leave until about 8.30 p.m.

Kate was looking forward to seeing Port Arthur. Her mother had visited Tasmania as a teenager and had absolutely loved it. Kate was interested in historic things and her mum, Wendy, had told her stories about Port Arthur.

The site of a convict prison to which more than 12,000 people were transported from 1831 to the 1870s, Port Arthur is a chilling and imposing reminder of Australia's colonial past. More than 200,000 people visit it each year. Tourism underpins the entire economy of the peninsula and its 2000 residents. Visitors are amazed by the beauty of the forty-hectare prison site, with its waterside setting, mellow stone ruins, meticulously restored cottages, beautiful gardens and tranquil atmosphere.

Port Arthur was chosen as the site for a penal settlement for repeat offenders because of its isolation and rich timber resources. There was easy access from Hobart down the Derwent and across Storm Bay, but the only land route from the Tasman Peninsula was across a narrow isthmus called Eaglehawk Neck, about 19 kilometres north of the prison site. Eaglehawk Neck was guarded by a military garrison and a line of savage dogs.

Convict transportation to Tasmania ended in 1853, but Port Arthur remained a prison for another twenty-four years. By then its population had dwindled to about 260, the majority of them paupers and lunatics. When the prison was closed in 1877, the last of the prisoners were moved to gaol in Hobart. When the prisoners, still fitted with leg-irons, arrived at the city wharf, they attracted a large crowd.

That year the prison settlement of Port Arthur was renamed Carnarvon, in a bid to remove its convict image. Then, late last century, one of the buildings was converted to a town hall and council chambers, and another became a hotel. Tasmania was sensitive about its convict beginnings (in 1857 a census revealed that 50 per cent of adult males were convicts or ex-convicts) and there was pressure to hide, or forget, the past as soon as possible. However, the grim fascination with the past remained and, soon after its closure, Port Arthur attracted its first tourists, most of whom came from Hobart by steamer. Some of the visitors were guided by ex-convicts who had drifted back to the area to eke out a living telling tall tales of their life under the lash.

The silent movie *For the Term of His Natural Life*, which was based on the book written in 1870 by Marcus Clarke, was produced on site in 1908. Its success focused further attention on the area. A bushfire that swept through Port Arthur in the summer of 1897 had gutted many of the buildings, including the Model Prison, and the ruins continued to deteriorate until the late 1970s, when a conservation and restoration program was begun.

The road from Hobart to Port Arthur wound through small townships and farmlands before reaching the Tasman Peninsula. Like most visitors, Mick, Kate, John and Caroline made a quick detour from Eaglehawk Neck past Pirates Bay to inspect the Blowhole, one of a series of spectacular coastal features formed by the pounding waves of the Tasman Sea. They took a few photos, then drove on to Port Arthur.

They arrived at the toll booth at about 12.30 p.m., but the thirteen-dollar entrance fee stopped them in their tracks. Mick and John were having second thoughts, but they were over-ruled by the two women: "Put your hand in your pocket and pay."

They did, and it was worth it. Port Arthur was at its best that day: fine, cool weather and no more than 600 or 700 people at the site.

Their first impression reminded them of an English park. Running down to Masons Cove, the grounds were dotted with giant oak trees and mellow stone and brick buildings. Across the water was a small island. At first glance, it was hard to imagine that this was once a grim prison settlement where convicts in leg-irons served out their time felling trees and sawing timber, building ships, making bricks and quarrying stone. At the bottom of the hill leading down from the toll booth was a village green, and to the right the splendid government gardens, which had been beautifully restored. Not until the guides introduce tourists to the solitary confinement cells, and outline the daily existence of the prisoners and the gaolers last century, does the past come alive.

Mick was conscious of the 4.15 airport departure, but realised that he and John had spent a lot of time with Darryl in the lead-up to the wedding, and there hadn't been much chance for Kate and Caroline to do anything more than some shopping. They were all keen to make up for the lost sightseeing opportunities. Kate wanted to see the convict coal mines at Saltwater River on the other side of the Tasman Peninsula. Coal had been discovered there in 1833, and the underground mines became a punishment station for hundreds of convicts from Port Arthur. Breaches of discipline among the miners earned a spell in underground solitary confinement cells, which can still be seen today.

Mick came up with a solution. It was Kate's day out, so he decided to phone the boss to see if he could get the next day off. That way they could change their flight and leave Hobart airport with John and Caroline about 8.30 p.m.

After arranging to meet the others in the Broad Arrow Café for some lunch, Mick and Kate set off to find a public phone. Things were quiet at the mine, Mick was told when he rang, so it would probably be all okay, but as the boss wasn't around, he'd be wise to phone back an hour and a half later.

It was looking good as they strolled into the Broad Arrow. A few metres behind them, a yellow Volvo with a surfboard on the roof stopped just outside the car park. It had entered the Port Arthur site just minutes before. Steven Howard, who was helping man the toll booth, had noticed the driver because the Volvo had had to reverse suddenly to avoid a minor bingle with a car in front. The other vehicle had rolled back before moving off down into the site. The Volvo's driver, who seemed to be a touch dazed or agitated, made some comment about the other driver's lack of skill.

Down by the parking areas near the Broad Arrow, the site's security officer, Ian Kingston, was doing his best to sort out the congestion. He spotted the Volvo, which had stopped at the bottom of the toll-booth road just where it intersected with Tarleton Street. Kingston walked across and asked the driver to do a U-turn and park further up the road. The driver, who was alone in the vehicle, appeared to be in his mid-twenties. His hair was long, and he wore a green jacket. There was a large multi-coloured "Prince" sports bag on the back seat. The driver appeared somewhat disgruntled about being asked to move.

Kingston wasn't surprised by the driver's attitude. The majority of visitors tended to park wherever they wanted. Their focus was on seeing the site and absorbing the history and heritage, not taking directions from attendants.

Soon after, Kingston noticed that the Volvo had been parked in front of the information office, adjacent to the Broad Arrow, and he saw the driver go into the office. After about a minute the young man walked out, got into the car and drove down to the water's edge, where he parked.

Some minutes later, Kingston saw the driver get out, open the driver's side rear door and pull out a sports bag. On one shoulder he carried a video camera. He closed the car door, walked towards the Broad Arrow, then went in.

An elderly South Australian couple, who were on a coach tour, came out of the Broad Arrow Cafe, heading for their bus. The woman could not help noticing the young man sitting at an outside table, eating hurriedly. He was virtually shovelling food into his mouth, as if he were starving. Beside him on a chair was a large multi-coloured sports bag.

"You have to look out for the European wasps here," he said to them as they passed. Then he added: "There's not many Japanese tourists around."

Inside the Broad Arrow, Mick, Kate and Caroline were seated at a table eating. John was at the servery.

It was then that Mick looked up and saw a young man with blond hair walk in and place what looked like a tennis bag on a nearby table.

PART 1

The Shadow

CHAPTER 2

The Firecracker Boy

Martin Bryant's arrival into the world was announced to the Tasmanian community in a notice in the classifieds of the Hobart *Mercury* on 9 May 1967:

> Bryant (Cordwell) – At Queen Alexandra Hospital on May 7, 1967, to Carleen and Maurice. A bouncing boy. Thanks to doctor and staff.

Like all new parents, the Bryants had high hopes for their son, and in 1973, after a year at preschool, Martin was enrolled at Hobart's prestigious private co-educational school, Friends'. Operated by the Quakers, Friends' had an excellent academic record, and its students regularly dominated university entrance awards.

But any dreams that Martin would add to that record were dashed very early. He was proving to be a handful at home, and in grade one at Friends' his behaviour was aggressive and destructive and his language skills poor. The following year he was given specialist assessment and teaching at an assessment centre. There appeared to be some improvement.

The Bryants decided to move young Martin from the fee-paying school and transfer him to New Town Primary School. Martin seemed excited at the prospect of changing schools. But by grade four he was in trouble again. He had no special friends and seemed to delight in disrupting the class. Most of the other children barely tolerated him, and he laughed off reprimands from teachers. Often they resorted to sending him from the room. Arts and craft were about the only lessons he appeared to enjoy. Later that year, the ten-year-old was given a two-day suspension.

Then followed another stint at a diagnostic and assessment centre, where learning difficulties were identified. Mention was made of Martin's need to be the centre of attention. For a brief time there was some improvement in his general behaviour, and he attended a school camp without incident. Teachers commented on his improvement. Although his classwork skills were low, the boy was trying.

Martin's final year of primary school was completed without any of the aggression of previous years, but he struggled with maths and reading and most other subjects, and was still without any close friends.

That year he was admitted to hospital in Hobart suffering from burns – caused, he said, when he had an accident while playing with fireworks – and he missed several weeks of schooling. A local television reporter recorded a bedside interview with him. What had he been doing, the interviewer asked? He had wanted to see if the wick would light, he replied. And it did.

"Will you be playing with fire crackers any more?" the interviewer inquired.

"Yes," he answered.

"And have you learned a lesson from this?"

"Yes, but I'm still playing with them," said the young Martin Bryant.

But others told another story, of a twelve-year-old Martin Bryant pouring petrol over himself and setting himself alight at a beach party at Carnarvon Bay, Port Arthur. Teenagers at the party had jumped on him and rolled him in the sand to extinguish the flames, then someone ran to the Bryant shack and called Martin's mother to the scene. Martin was then taken to hospital. He had often carried a small, green, square can of petrol with him, and would threaten to throw petrol in the camp fire at beach parties. "Here comes silly Martin with his can," the other kids would say.

Martin's secondary school years were spent in special opportunity classes at New Town High School, an all-boys high school in Hobart. The classes were for the kids who couldn't cope with mainstream schooling because they were intellectually slow, or who had behavioural problems and were disruptive.

An early report was cautiously optimistic about the boy who had arrived with a reputation for being aggressive and a slow learner. It noted he had settled in quite well to the environment at New Town High, but had a few social problems to overcome.

Martin was antagonistic to other students and seemed to

have difficulties interacting. However, for a year or so he worked reasonably well in some subjects. Then he began to lose interest again. He also began, occasionally, to lose his temper.

His two years in the senior opportunity group provided Martin with perhaps the most stable environment of his entire school career. The class was small – about eighteen students – and the male teacher, an experienced hand, was sensitive but firm with his charges. There was some freedom, but everybody knew the guidelines.

To his teacher, it was obvious very early on that Martin was different, one of a kind. "A slow learner and not, to use the old terminology, retarded," the teacher said. Martin wasn't thick; he wasn't bright, but he wasn't thick. But he *was* lazy; he didn't really want to work at any sort of academic subject.

The most worrying thing about the teenager, thought his teacher, was that he was the most socially isolated youngster he had ever taught. Martin had no ability to connect with other people. He shrank back within himself, rarely spoke, and had no friends. The other boys called him "the shadow", because he moved so quietly and had an unnerving knack of suddenly appearing and never speaking.

The only classes in which the isolated youngster showed any interest were woodwork and art. As was reasonable with his hands, he could work alone. But attempts to involve Martin in group situations in the classroom always failed.

The boy would never let you know what he was feeling; his eyes would go blank as if he wasn't there. There was a lot going on behind those steely blue eyes, but you could never get it to come out.

One of the teacher's ploys to improve classroom contact was to encourage the boys to talk about what they had done at weekends. Martin never volunteered any information, but the others could occasionally pressure him into some brief disclosure, simply by keeping at him, asking, taunting. His teacher heard from a couple of the other kids that Martin had claimed he had tortured an echidna. Apart from that it was known that Martin's favourite possession was his spear gun. It was his pride and joy, and he loved going to the family shack at Port Arthur to go skindiving.

One boy at the school did count himself a friend of Martin Bryant. Greg Lahey was the same age as Martin, and the two boys became good friends when they were about fourteen years old. They stayed at each other's homes, and Greg would visit the Bryant shack at Carnarvon Bay. At times, to Greg, Martin seemed "off the planet" and became vague and would mumble to himself, but Greg regarded him as a close friend.

Martin did behave oddly at times: on one occasion when the boys were walking to the Bryant house in Lenah Valley, Martin had picked up a cat and had begun trying to pull it apart with his bare hands. Greg knew that Martin hated cats, but he forced Bryant to set the terrified animal free. Then, on a floundering trip near Nubeena with his father, Maurice, Martin thrust a flounder spear towards Greg's feet as if trying to stab him. Bryant seemed to think it was a huge joke, but Maurice Bryant made him apologise. More chillingly, on three separate occasions while Lahey was staying with the family at Carnarvon Bay, Bryant pointed an air rifle at him and pulled the trigger. The gun was always unloaded but, badly frightened, Lahey had no way of knowing that, and it seemed Martin enjoyed his reaction.

Their friendship finally ended in 1981 when the two boys went diving off the Tasman Peninsula. Greg was swimming towards the surface to get air when he felt a sharp jab on the top of his head. He looked up to see Bryant with a spear. Lahey's wetsuit had saved him from injury, but he was so angry he punched Martin when they reached the shore. Still Martin seemed to regard the incident as a joke, and Greg Lahey had nothing more to do with him from that day on.

Neither of Martin's parents attended parent–teacher nights, though his teacher spoke a few times on the phone to Mrs Bryant. Martin was difficult to manage, his mother said. His teacher believed that Martin disliked his father, Maurice. There appeared to be no rapport between them. But Martin seemed to get on all right with his mum.

Martin's remoteness continued out in the hurly burly of the schoolground at recess and lunchtimes. Other kids sometimes taunted him, but Martin was so different from them he was able to walk away from it. His ability to withdraw totally from his surroundings was his protection.

Martin could be seen in the playground, wandering, totally alone, and seemingly almost happy to be so. He did have quite a good sense of humour and a cackling laugh. Slapstick and situation comedy – simplistic humour – was what he enjoyed most. But there was never any real warmth from him.

The remote world of Martin Bryant worried staff at the school. They were keen to try to get him into some sort of social grouping where he could mix with people, because even when he was in the "forced" environment of the school he still didn't relate to other people. Occasionally he was aggressive towards the other boys, but it was never much more than lashing out with a fist and a curse. Most of his fellow students would have acted similarly under the circumstances.

More often than not, though, Martin Bryant would close off from the other student and, instead of hitting him, fix him with an angry, steely glare. It was a glare which suggested a grudge had been born and that it was being filed away. This pent-up aggression worried his teachers. When he looked in anger at anyone who had done something to him, he seemed to be harbouring a deep-seated resentment that he was building up and might use against someone at a later time. He didn't make threats, but his look felt deadly.

The boy needed an outlet, but wasn't the sort of kid that should have done judo or tae kwon do, because he might have used it in the wrong way.

It seemed that society was an alien world to Martin Bryant. Neither the educational situation nor the social situation suited him. Nor did they do him much good. At least the support and structure of the special education unit was better for him than the open learning environment, which would have been disastrous. What other alternative could have been offered to Martin Bryant?

CHAPTER 3

....

The Heiress's Heir

Tasmania is home to several members of an elite club. They are a fortunate few, people who never need to worry about where the next dollar is coming from, and certainly don't need to have a flutter on the lotteries in the hope of getting rich. They are the beneficiaries of the will of George Adams, the founder of Tattersalls lotteries.

George Adams brought his lottery business to Tasmania from Queensland just before the turn of the century. He died in Hobart in 1904. Having no children, he left the bulk of his estate to a nephew, and small shares to various company officials and staff members. The details of the bequests have always been kept secret, but the money has flowed to Tasmanian families ever since.

One of the beneficiaries was David Hastie Harvey, Adams's general manager, who died in Hobart in 1927. His share was passed down through his family, and eventually at least part of it – possibly as much as $150,000 a year –

reached David Hastie Harvey's grand-daughter, Helen Mary Harvey.

Born in Hobart in May 1933, the only child of Lorimer (a son of David Harvey) and Hilza Harvey, Helen never married. Much of her adult life was spent caring for her parents in their imposing two-storey house on a large block at 30 Clare Street, New Town, in inner suburban Hobart.

Helen, a robust and eccentric character, worked for a short time as a clerk with the Tasmanian Government Railways, but after the death of her father in the 1980s, devoted herself to looking after her invalid mother. Helen had two great joys in her life. The first was animals, particularly dogs and cats, and the house was over-run with them. Her second love was videos: *The Sound of Music, A Star is Born, Random Harvest, Gentlemen Prefer Blondes, Seven Brides for Seven Brothers, The Swiss Family Robinson*. She would buy dozens of movies at a time.

As the years went on, the extensive grounds of 30 Clare Street, with their greenhouse and fish pond, became overgrown and jungle-like. The neighbours looked on, wondered and occasionally complained to the council about the mess – and the smell.

Generally, though, Helen Harvey was accepted for what she was – a real eccentric, happy within her world, and pleasant and cheerful to anyone she met. She was the funny lady who adopted animals by the dozen, the lady with the Tatts money who had more than she would ever need.

In the early months of 1987 she decided to hire someone to do gardening and other odd jobs. She hired nineteen-year-old Martin Bryant. He was living just half a kilometre away with his parents, Maurice and Carleen, and his young sister, Lindy. The neighbours joked that gardening at 30 Clare Street would be a lifetime occupation, given the way it had grown unchecked for decades.

Martin was still a loner. At home, his parents struggled to control his behaviour. They tried to ensure that one of them was with him at all times. After Martin had left school, aged sixteen, his father, Maurice, a waterside worker in Hobart for thirty years, sought to keep his son occupied with part-time gardening and other odd jobs.

Martin also sold vegetables door to door. Most of his customers thought the young man was a little strange, simple perhaps, but he was polite and he liked to talk.

Sadly, though, Martin's life was going nowhere. He had been assessed as an invalid pensioner when he was eighteen because it was determined there was no prospect of him ever being able to gain or maintain full-time employment. His was a life without status, and he was a person who had never been able to develop long-lasting relationships or to really feel a part of society

But at 30 Clare Street, Martin Bryant found not only an employer in the wealthy and bizarre Helen Harvey, but a friend. She lavished gifts on him. She also gave him some control and direction. "For Martin, she's a bit like a sergeant major," one neighbour had commented.

About the middle of 1990, Martin, then twenty-three, came to live in the house with the dozens of dogs and cats and Miss Harvey. He quit his family home after a clash with his father, and Helen Harvey took him under her wing.

Strangers assumed he was her son, and they became a familiar sight in and around Hobart – the eccentric and occasionally boisterous middle-aged "Tatts lady" and the young man with the polite manner and the piercing blue eyes.

Martin learnt that, when Helen Harvey died, he was to inherit everything. The house itself, the farm, cash, art works, furnishings, even the hundreds of videos she had bought over the years. All up it came to more than one million dollars. For a young man classified in his late teens as an invalid pensioner, unable to work, it was beyond imagination.

In her will, Harvey referred to Martin as "her dear friend" and directed that when he, too, died, he be buried beside her. As well as showering Martin with gifts, she took him and his family to Hobart's best restaurants. The strange and indulgent world she had created at 30 Clare Street was probably the happiest environment Martin Bryant had ever known.

It was certainly strange. In June 1990 an ambulance crew which called at 30 Clare Street to take Helen and her mother, Hilza, to hospital, found an extraordinary scene. The two women were living in the kitchen of the large house amid terrible squalor, and it was obvious that dozens of dogs and cats had the run of the place. The old woman was bed-ridden and her daughter, who had cared for her for years, had a hip problem which restricted her own mobility, so both beds had been moved into the kitchen.

There was food in a bowl in the microwave oven on a bench, and mould had grown out of the bowl and reached the top of the oven. Saucepans sitting in the kitchen had been there for a long, long time. It was both saddening and bizarre to enter such a large house and find two people living only in the kitchen. The room was so crowded it was impossible to walk across the floor to reach Hilza Harvey in her bed. Instead, the ambulance workers had to clamber across the beds and other furniture.

Hilza Harvey was quite lucid and chatted to the ambulancemen as they prepared to transfer her to the vehicle. In every way, the conversations that day were quite normal; it just appeared that these two people had different priorities.

Hilza Harvey told one ambulance officer that they had a nice young man who came in and looked after them.

"I don't think you're getting very good value for your money," was his dry response.

Despite their problems, neither woman would leave their home until arrangements had been made to care for their pets. They were determined that someone look after all the animals, so the ambulance workers arranged for the police to call in the RSPCA.

The RSPCA officials found twenty-six cats in a shed behind the house, seventeen dogs living in the house, one occupying a station wagon, and two others in another vehicle. There were dog faeces and hair throughout the house.

Hobart City Council issued a clean-up order, and Martin and his father did the job. They used a garden hoe to scrape encrusted grime and filth from the kitchen floorboards. The task of complying with the council direction took them a month, and skip-loads of rubbish were carted to the tip.

It was not the first time that the Harveys had come under council notice. In November 1988 they had been ordered to clear up the overgrown garden, which had been labelled a fire hazard. The work was done, but in January 1990 health officials were called following a complaint from a neighbour about a strong smell. The officials found more than thirty cats in a shed, and later learned there were twenty dogs, fifteen of which lived inside the house. Miss Harvey was told to reduce the number of animals kept on the property.

Helen's love of pets was well known to neighbours and visiting tradesmen. For Wayne Wright, who had the Mount Stuart Butchery in Elphinstone Road for several years from the late 1970s to early 1980s, Helen was his best customer. She would call in to the shop, less than a kilometre from 30 Clare Street, twice a week, or phone in an order and he would deliver. After buying some meat for herself and her mother, she would ask for a full rump (five to eight kilograms) or a full topside (seven to ten kilograms) to be cut up for her dogs and cats. It was always cash – up to $120 a week – and he never had to send her an account. To the butcher, Miss Harvey was a wonderful customer and a lovely lady with a sense of humour, always happy to chat about her dogs or the football.

Wright called at 30 Clare Street on a few occasions, and he estimated that there were fifteen or twenty cats, and at least a dozen dogs. The dogs had their own rooms and real beds. She showed the butcher through the house one day, introducing him to the dogs and pointing out their various rooms. He didn't know which way to look. It was all a bit odd.

But the butcher's relationship with Helen Harvey ended in strange circumstances. Making a home delivery one week, Wright walked down the path through Helen Harvey's overgrown garden and saw what he thought was a snake. When she answered the door, he told her what he had seen.

She became very concerned and told him he must not risk walking up the path again. Instead she would call at his shop. He never heard from her again.

Helen Harvey, sometimes with Martin beside her, was a popular figure among car dealers, and bought and sold up to fifty vehicles during her lifetime. One car salesman remembered the two arriving together, and Martin pointing to the car he wanted and saying, "That's nice. I'll have that one." Miss Harvey had then paid for it in cash.

Some cars were bought and sold again within a few weeks. On one occasion a purchase lasted just five hours before it was swapped. The vehicles were often sold at a considerable loss. One was reversed into a tree and dented and scratched, so Miss Harvey and Martin carried out their own repairs, using house paint, before reselling it. The dogs that occupied the cars did their share in forcing down resale values by devouring the upholstery and fouling the interiors.

On 27 July 1990, Helen Harvey's mother, Hilza, died and was buried at Cornelian Bay cemetery in Hobart.

CHAPTER 4

On the Road to Port Arthur

In late 1991, Martin Bryant and Helen Harvey moved to a farm at Copping, south of Hobart on the road to Port Arthur.

The menagerie of dogs and cats was expanded to include horses and miniature horses, and even a pig. The new residents' husbandry practices both amazed and amused the local farmers: the pig was said to share a room with Martin. One farmer saw horses standing in a bare paddock, while the paddock next to them was green. It didn't make a lot of sense.

And, almost immediately, there was trouble with the neighbours, the Featherstones. Barry Featherstone, a farmer, and his brother, John, a works supervisor at the Port Arthur Historic Site, lived on separate properties adjoining the Copping farm. They soon discovered that Martin Bryant was a very strange character indeed. John's wife and sixteen-year-old daughter went to the farm to introduce themselves and to inquire whether they could buy raspberries from them, as they had done from the previous owner. Miss Harvey invited them into the house and told Martin to make them all a cup of tea. He did, then disappeared, but returned before they had a chance to drink it.

Martin told them they had to leave. "Take no notice of him," Miss Harvey said. With that, the two women finished their tea, said goodbye, and walked down the pathway leading from the house. It was then that they heard a voice: "Don't ever come back here, or I'll shoot the two of you." It was Martin. The two women were badly shocked, and they hurried home.

John Featherstone advised his family to avoid Bryant and Harvey. Realising Martin was simple, he decided there was no point confronting the young man, and it would be best not to stir him up.

In the months to follow, however, Featherstone became so concerned about Bryant that he relayed a message to the effect that, if he ever set foot on the Featherstone property, that would be it. Bryant was in the habit of roaming around the area at night, and occasionally, during the day, he fired a few shots from what sounded like a small-calibre gun.

Miss Harvey told her neighbour that Bryant was living with her because he couldn't get on with his father and had threatened to shoot him. She said that she thought the best thing to do was to separate them.

Featherstone's concern extended to warning his son, a TAFE student, to avoid Bryant if he saw him waiting for the bus to Hobart. On the occasions Featherstone's son and Bryant met at the stop there were no problems. But once Bryant was on the bus he changed, annoying and harassing girls. Some drivers put him off. Others drove past, refusing to pick him up. Bryant would chase the bus, cursing and swearing.

When Barry Featherstone, John's brother, visited the Harvey farm to ask if they needed any contracting work done, he was met at the back door by Bryant.

"Get out of here!" yelled Bryant, and pushed the other man in the chest.

There was a struggle before Featherstone ran back to his car, got in and drove off quickly. As the shocked farmer pulled into his own drive, Bryant pulled up alongside.

"Don't you ever set foot in my place again," he shouted, "or I'll call the police! And I'll call my lawyer, too!"

Featherstone was staggered. He tried to reason with Bryant, eventually climbing into Bryant's car and sitting beside him. Bryant's response was to burst into tears. Featherstone told him to leave. As Bryant left, he yelled that he'd shoot Featherstone.

Shortly afterwards, Helen Harvey drove up with Bryant in the passenger seat. Harvey got out of the car and apologised to Featherstone. Bryant said nothing, but shook his hand.

Featherstone knew he had a peculiar neighbour, but things improved enough for him to do some work for them, and he spoke to Bryant occasionally.

On 20 October 1992, Helen Harvey was killed in a road smash less than 2 kilometres from Copping, which was midway between Hobart and Port Arthur. Her car was on the wrong side of the road when it collided with another vehicle. Bryant, the passenger, was seriously injured in the accident and had to be cut from the wreck by ambulance officers.

The two had been at Sorell buying groceries and feed for their livestock, and Bryant said later that his last memory before the crash was of turning his head because three dogs were fighting in the back seat. Harvey and Bryant always travelled with some of their animals.

The Bryant family – Maurice and Carleen, Martin and Lindy – together with other friends of Miss Harvey, placed a death notice in the Hobart *Mercury* which included a short verse.

> From quiet homes and first beginning,
> Out to undiscovered ends,
> There's nothing worth the wear of winning,
> But laughter and the love of friends.

It was the second accident Helen and Martin had been involved in that year. The first, close to the same scene, happened at night. Bryant had said that their car had been hit from the rear by another vehicle after Harvey had braked to avoid a kangaroo lying on the road. There were no injuries.

Although Helen Harvey's death was found to be accidental, the finger was pointed at Bryant. After all, she was said to have told neighbours that she always drove slowly because Bryant would sometimes yank the steering wheel. "Oh, he's a worry to me sometimes," Helen Harvey had told Neil Noye, a farmer and the mayor of Tasman Council, when she and Bryant had visited him at his farm near Nubeena to inquire about buying cattle. "He grabbed hold of the steering wheel coming down today and nearly pulled me off the road, going silly. What would you do with him?"

Helen Harvey's death meant that Martin Bryant was a

wealthy young man, but authorities didn't consider him capable of managing his assets. Following an application by his mother late in 1993, Perpetual Trustees were appointed by a court to manage his financial affairs.

Despite his newfound affluence, Bryant remained friendless and isolated. Recovering from his injuries in Hobart, Bryant told a taxi driver that he had been injured in a skiing accident and had decided to give the sport away.

During Bryant's recuperation, his father moved on to the farm and took over the running of it. Maurice Bryant disposed of most of the animals, either by shooting or selling them. Martin would not be returning, he said, and things seemed to operate smoothly for a while. But Martin did return.

On Monday, 16 August 1993, Maurice Bryant was found dead in a dam on the Copping farm. Maurice, sixty-four, a retired waterside worker, had a history of depression. He had driven from his home in Hobart to the farm on the morning of 13 August. He had phoned his wife at their home in Lenah Valley from the farm at Copping, at about seven o'clock that night.

About 10 a.m. the next day, Constable Garry Whittle, of Dunalley police, went to the farm after being informed that a note, apparently written by Maurice Bryant, had been found on the door of the farmhouse. "Call the police," it read. The note had been found by a person who called at the farm to collect a trailer that had been advertised for sale. There was no-one else at the farm when the visitor arrived.

Volunteers, including members of the Dunalley Fire Brigade, began a search of the property, and several thousand dollars were found in a bag in a vehicle.

Assisted by trainees from the Police Academy, the police search and rescue squad took over the search. When the land search was unsuccessful, divers began to check the numerous small dams on the property. While searching around the farmhouse and outbuildings on Monday, 16 August, one police trainee noticed a young fellow with blond hair, watching intently from the fence line. He asked a colleague who the young man was, and was told it was the missing man's son, Martin.

Other searchers returned to the farm buildings. Martin hung around the edge of the group and, seemingly unconcerned about the fate of his father, he approached some policewomen and tried to start up a conversation.

Then Maurice's body was found, at the bottom of a deep dam. It had a weight belt strapped across it like a bandolier. Constable Whittle took Martin to the scene to identify his father. The searchers were amazed to see Martin walking back from the dam, laughing. The young man must suffer from some form of mental illness, they decided.

While other police went down to the dam to inspect the scene, Martin was heard laughing and joking as the local water carrier filled the farm tanks. The searchers had lunch before returning to the Police Academy, and again Martin tried to chat to some of the policewomen.

John Featherstone also noticed that the young man did not appear upset, but instead spent much of the time brush-cutting grass along a boundary fence while the search was in progress. News of Martin's strange reaction spread and fuelled the rumours that had begun with Helen Harvey's death.

Martin could have been responsible for his father's

death, people said When, on 18 July of the following year, the coroner found that Maurice Bryant had died by drowning, consistent with suicide, the finding did little to assuage the suspicions of some of the locals.

John Featherstone, for one, remained deeply suspicious of the circumstances surrounding Maurice Bryant's demise and the road accident which had claimed Helen Harvey's life on the highway a short distance from the farm in October 1992. He remembered that, on the same night that Harvey was killed and Martin Bryant seriously injured, Martin's father, Maurice, had arrived about ten o'clock and moved in.

In August 1993, some people John Featherstone had never met before asked him whether he knew a man named Martin, or anything about a horse float being advertised for sale. The price sounded too good to be true, they felt, but Featherstone was able to assure them it was in an as-new condition. When they had asked Martin why he was selling, he had replied that his father had recently passed away, the strangers told Featherstone.

"I saw Maurice just this morning!" Featherstone had remarked to his wife, after telling her the story. "I said g'day to him over the bloody fence." A couple of days later, Featherstone heard that Maurice Bryant had been found dead.

Martin Bryant had lost two of the most influential people in his life within the space of a year and now the community was suggesting he had killed them. Not for the first time, Martin Bryant felt a deep sense of rejection.

CHAPTER 5

A Separate World

After the inquest into the death of Helen Harvey was completed in early 1993, Martin moved back into 30 Clare Street in New Town, Hobart. The house behind was home to the Kuiper family, who were newcomers to the neighbourhood. No-one saw more closely into Martin Bryant's world of fantasy, child-like behaviour and loneliness than Harry and Anitra Kuiper and their three children. When the Kuipers moved in, 30 Clare Street was empty. One day, Anitra Kuiper was hanging out the washing after the kids had gone to school when suddenly she heard a voice from behind: "Oh hello. I'm Martin."

It gave her quite a scare, because she hadn't heard him approaching the fence. When she turned around, the man before her struck her as strange. She didn't say anything and just walked away.

Five or six weeks after Anitra first saw Bryant over the

fence, they met again and talked. He was, she thought, a bit simple, and it was difficult to sustain a conversation because he didn't communicate and converse like a normal person. Half the time he'd ignore a question and go on about something totally unrelated. There was never a logical flow. But, for all that, he seemed a happy, casual sort of a fellow. Certainly no threat to anybody. Just a bit odd.

One evening, Harry Kuiper went to Bryant's front door to say hello and seek permission to get onto Bryant's property so he could repair their side fence. The lights were on as he approached the door, but were flicked off as he knocked, and there was no answer. Bryant told Anitra later that he didn't like answering the door after dark. It sounded like a lame excuse, particularly from an adult male.

The Kuipers had a discussion as to how they should deal with their neighbour and decided that the Christian approach would be to treat him just like anybody else, until they found anything to indicate otherwise. For more than a year the Kuiper family were friends to Martin Bryant, despite the stories other residents told of his irrational outbursts and generally odd behaviour.

Their neighbour seemed to live in a separate world, a world quite different from everyone else's. It was a bizarre world, where Martin wrote to a primary school head teacher asking if he could enrol in the same class as the Kuipers's daughter, who was then in grade six. It was a world where, in his late twenties, he would socialise with the three Kuiper children, aged thirteen, eleven and nine, as equals. Martin was just the biggest kid in the group, with a sense of fun and a generous nature.

It was a world where Bryant would prepare his evening meal at five o'clock and be in bed, lights out, at eight-thirty.

Yes, the Kuipers knew from others in the area that Martin could become aggressive and irrational if he felt his privacy or his property was being invaded. There were stories of blazing rows over the trimming of overhanging trees, and shouts and threats that he would call his lawyer.

But the Kuiper children found him fun, fascinating and very generous. They all made trips into the city and to Salamanca Place, a popular shopping spot. He was proud to have such friends. Martin would walk up to strangers and say: "I'm taking these guys to Salamanca, and then we're going to the movies . . . and I bought them an icecream." With Anitra, the Kuiper kids were taken to afternoon tea to Hobart's five-star dockside hotel, the Sheraton.

Among his favourite possessions was a "talking" Bart Simpson doll which he delighted in demonstrating. On one occasion Martin went to K-mart and bought four large water pistols for $26 each. There was one for each of them, and one for himself, so they could stage water pistol battles in the overgrown front garden of 30 Clare Street. The Kuiper children were showered with such gifts.

It was as if Martin Bryant was struggling to find a purpose and a place for his life, to gain some recognition and admiration. But all his efforts would be fantasy, or child-like, and he would never understand why others either laughingly dismissed him, or ignored him.

Martin's mother, Carleen, once phoned Anitra and warned her not to allow the children to travel in the car with Martin. She gave no reasons, but repeated the warning. Anitra was instructed not to tell anyone else, especially Martin. There was a subsequent call, and Mrs Bryant said the children should not be friends with Martin. She gave an excuse that there was a broken pane in the greenhouse at Martin's place. Anitra knew there wasn't, but she took the advice about the car, assuming that Martin might be one of those people who showed off if others were in the car with him. Still, she felt that there was something more behind the warning; that something was being hidden from them.

The Kuiper children were free to roam through Bryant's rambling house. Anitra allowed them to visit Clare Street, together, and for no more than twenty minutes at a time, and Bryant occasionally returned to Bedford Street with them. Anitra had a golden rule never to allow her kids to be alone with an adult male, but she thought that Martin was a bit of an exception.

For the children it was a marvellous adventure – Martin had "excellent" things. But their keen eyes also spotted a dead rat in a window and the kitty litter trays, uncleaned, in some of the rooms.

However, it was a far cry from the squalor in which Helen Harvey had lived her last years with her menagerie of pets. The fouled and stained carpets had been removed and replaced with new floor coverings and, if the place wasn't quite *Home Beautiful*, it was a vast improvement on what it had been.

There was still ample evidence of the eccentric lifestyle of Helen Harvey: the disabled electric appliances, particularly TV sets, scattered about the house, their cords chewed through by the dogs which used to live indoors. It was as if she hadn't cared, and certainly hadn't bothered with repairs. If the dogs damaged a TV set, she had just gone out and bought another.

The children once found two unused CD players still in their boxes. They were identical. "Take the one you want," said Martin. The children were his friends, after all. A portable TV set was another gift.

But there were two places that Bryant would not allow the children access to, no matter how inquisitive they became. One was the padlocked cupboard under the stairs, and the other was under the house itself. They asked him what was under the stairs but he wouldn't tell them.

Only once did Martin become very angry and threaten violence. He told Anitra that his mother was planning to move into the house with him. He was furious, and went wild. Anitra told him it was no good telling her how he felt. The sensible thing to do would be to tell his mother and, if he didn't want her to move in, he should tell her so.

Bryant responded angrily: "I'll kill her if she moves in with me. She's always telling me what to do, and I'll have to do all this stuff that I don't want to do."

Anitra dismissed the threat as just something that had spilled out because he was so worked up. In any case, it was hardly unusual that a man in his late twenties would want to keep his independence. Two or three weeks later they heard that Mrs Bryant had bought another house and moved away from the area.

Martin had told the Kuipers that he hadn't liked his father and, when asked by Anitra what had happened to Maurice Bryant, he replied: "Oh, he died of a heart attack in my mother's living room."

But Bryant's friendship with the Kuiper children was

ended after he started to act possessively towards the thirteen-year-old Kuiper girl, and showed the children pornography. Bryant had suggested a game of cards and produced a pack with pornographic pictures on the backs.

When Harry Kuiper told Martin the friendship and the association with the family was over, Martin couldn't understand what was happening. "Oh, my mother's been ringing you up, hasn't she? It's all her fault," he fumed.

"No, Martin. We really like you, you're very generous to the kids, but we can't have you showing them pornography. It's not anything your mother has done. It's what *you* did."

But Bryant wouldn't accept it, and over the next few months he tried desperately to restore the relationship, on one occasion knocking on the front door with a bunch of flowers for Anitra, on another, asking if he could take the daughter out to dinner. Whenever he saw the children in the street he would greet them and say things like: "Hey, we must get together some day."

But the Kuiper kids were no longer his friends, and Martin, again, was alone.

CHAPTER 6

The Frequent Flier

In his will, Maurice Bryant had left his superannuation, worth $250,000, to his son, adding to the wealth Martin had inherited from Helen Harvey. Almost immediately, Martin had embarked on a whirlwind of international and interstate travel.

In just three years he travelled out of Australia at least ten times, with the United Kingdom, Europe, the United States, Scandinavia, Malaysia and New Zealand figuring in his itineraries. His interstate schedule was no less hectic, with up to seven or eight trips a year. He enjoyed five-star hotels and dressed smartly, occasionally flamboyantly.

Martin Bryant was someone to be noticed. Unfortunately, however, it was often for the wrong reasons.

His approaches to women worried and annoyed many. "Would you like to come and have dinner with me?" was his standard pick-up line. His request for a woman's telephone number sometimes might succeed, though more often than not he was ignored or given a wrong number.

There were times when he obviously set out to shock or offend women. Waitresses and female shop assistants in Hobart knew him as "loopy", and were reluctant to serve him. A waitress at a leading Hobart hotel was asked about the icecream on the dessert menu. Out of hearing of anyone else, Bryant then said he would like to lick it from her body.

He once approached a heavily pregnant woman standing in Hobart's Centrepoint shopping centre and stroked her belly while she was window-shopping, then laughed at her startled reaction. Eventually he was barred from one suburban shopping centre.

Yet he could be charming, if odd. A 23-year-old Hobart female law student sat next to him for part of the time on a flight back from London. Before the plane took off, Bryant told her that he had informed his mother, in a phone call from the airport, that he had met the girl he was going to marry. Although the woman didn't feel threatened by him, she thought it strange when he mentioned he had gone to Disneyland but had come home after three days when it started raining. She sensed something was odd when he said he had a big house, and that she could move in with him.

During the 24-hour flight back from London to Melbourne, Bryant was very intense. He had been stunned by his father's death three years before and had not worked since, he said. In fact, Martin Bryant had never had a job, or certainly nothing more than his part-time gardening chores and vegetable-selling door to door. At various times he described himself as a carpenter or a farmer.

By 1995, Martin Bryant had found a girlfriend, Janetta,

who was seventeen. They had met because their mothers attended the same church in Hobart's northern suburbs and were acquaintances. While on a boating trip south of Hobart, shortly before a holiday in Surfers Paradise, Martin and Janetta had had to be rescued from their dinghy by the skipper of a fishing boat. Bryant had ignored the rough seas and Janetta's pleas to turn back. He seemed to show no fear at all.

Janetta decided to end the relationship when they returned home from a trip to Surfers Paradise. She felt he was behaving oddly. After the break-up they ran into each other from time to time around town, and Martin would ask her if she wanted to have dinner with him. Janetta always refused.

Martin was a member of Ansett Australia's frequent-flier club, who usually travelled business class, and he was well known to travel agents and booking clerks in Hobart. One Ansett staffer recalled that the first time she met him was when he came into the Hobart office and bought a discount ticket, then returned some time later saying he wanted to change it.

"You realise that it will cost you additional money," she pointed out to him.

"Don't worry about it," he said.

It was far from the usual client reaction to being asked to hand over more money. Bryant returned the following day and paid an additional $150 in cash. When the woman sympathised with him for having to part with the extra money, he said it didn't matter and then went on to add that he had taken twelve months off university. Isn't he lucky, she thought.

On another occasion, Bryant called in to the office to inquire about the regulations governing the carriage of guns and ammunition on planes. The woman was cautious, and suggested he ring the staff at the airport to ensure he received accurate information. Bryant didn't appear to be concerned or disappointed by that suggestion. On that occasion, as on others, he was quiet and polite.

The authorities also began to take notice of Martin on his travels. In early 1994, he was noticed acting oddly in Hereford in the United Kingdom. He had booked into an expensive hotel and paid in cash for a room, even though his general appearance suggested he was in no way affluent. Within a few minutes he startled the reception desk staff by announcing that the room was too hot and he was checking out. When he was offered a full refund, he waved it away, telling the staff they could keep it as a tip.

Later, he booked into a small guest house, but his strange behaviour had already been reported: Hereford is the home base of Britain's crack anti-terrorism force, the SAS, and is very security conscious. The report resulted in Interpol contacting the Tasmania police, wanting to know what was known about Martin Bryant. Nothing was, save that he had been fined for driving without a licence. Otherwise, his slate was clean.

But it wasn't the end of official interest in his travels, because when he arrived back in Australia a few days later, after a quick visit to the United States, some of his bags went astray and arrived at Melbourne airport as unaccompanied luggage. When Customs examined them they found and seized four pornographic videos depicting bestiality.

And then, in January 1996, Martin came under

surveillance after landing back in Melbourne from yet another trip to London. Something about him suggested that he might have drugs concealed on, or in, his body. Bryant agreed to a search and was taken to the Royal Melbourne Hospital. An X-ray showed he was innocent.

Martin Bryant was getting the attention he seemed to crave, but it seemed to be for all the wrong reasons.

CHAPTER 7

"I'll Think of Something..."

For years Nancy D'Alton had noticed Martin around the neighbourhood of New Town. From time to time she would meet him in the street, or see him having coffee in a milk bar or café in North Hobart's shopping precinct. He always looked lonely, so she would sit down and have a coffee with him and a chat. She felt that he suffered inwardly from disappointment and loneliness, and knew how that could eat away at a person.

In April 1996 they met outside the Purity supermarket in North Hobart, where she was waiting for a taxi.

"Come on a picnic with me this weekend," Martin said, and added that sometimes he didn't know what to do with himself. "We could go for a nice drive and I could take you to lunch. I'll show you where Miss Harvey had her property. You knew Miss Harvey, didn't you?"

Mrs D'Alton refused the invitation, explaining she was

committed to seeing her grandchildren at the weekend. But as she said it, she could see that something was wrong. Martin looked cross.

"Oh, I don't know. Nobody ever wants to listen to me, or go with me," he said. "I'm getting fed up with this. I'll think of something, I'll think of something, and everybody will remember me."

Mrs D'Alton was about to ask him not to get upset, and to assure him she would go with him if she could. But Martin Bryant was hurt and angry. He didn't stop to listen. Instead, he hurried away towards his yellow Volvo with the surfboard on top.

In mid-April, Martin went on a shopping trip into the city with his new girlfriend, Petra.

Martin went into a store and took out a tape measure. He began measuring large sports bags, telling Petra he needed one for Tai Chi. He was particularly interested in the length of bags and the strength of the handles, saying that he was worried the handles would tear. It had to be a strong bag, he told the sales person, as it was to hold ammunition. Finally he chose one and paid for it. It was a large sports bag, multi-coloured, in an eyecatching blend of blue, green, black and red, with the brand name "Prince" in bold white lettering on the side.

Days later, Bryant told Petra that he had decided against doing Tai Chi. She never saw the bag again.

Petra was a twenty-year-old TAFE student. She had met Martin Bryant a couple of months earlier, when she responded to an advertisement he placed for a gardener for 30 Clare Street. The Martin that Petra knew was a gentle person. He was never violent and, even when he was angry, was never verbally abusive. He liked action videos with plenty of gunplay in them, and Steven Seagal and Jackie Chan were among his favourite stars. There were hundreds of videos in the house at Clare Street, and Martin's favourites included *Platoon, Missing in Action, Under Siege, Halloween 4* and *Lone Wolf McQuaid.* There were also about a dozen pornographic movies.

Although he often talked about guns and his wish to be involved in some action, Petra never saw any weapons in the house. And, even though he loved to watch action videos, Martin had walked out of a movie at Hobart's Cinema Centre when he found one scene too violent. The movie was *Casino,* and the scene that upset him showed a man having his fingers crushed.

On Anzac Day, 1996, Bryant went with Petra to Richmond. The couple had lunch at the Wine Centre in the historic village's main street. Richmond is less than 30 kilometres north-east of Hobart, and was once a convict station. There is a gaol there that pre-dates Port Arthur by about five years. Today the village retains much of its colonial past and charm, with many of its 1840s-era buildings now housing tea rooms, art galleries and craft shops. Another of Richmond's major attractions is the bridge spanning the Coal River. Completed in 1825, it is the oldest in Australia, and the river banks are a popular picnic spot.

Martin wanted to try out his camera, and he took a photograph of two tourists having lunch beside the bridge. He had an odd habit of walking up to complete strangers and asking them questions about themselves: where they came from, what they did, where they were going. When the tourists, one Dutch and one German, declined his offer of a lift back to town, he seemed irritated, and as he walked away he remarked that they were silly people.

The following day, Friday, Petra and Martin had lunch at Salamanca Place in Hobart. A terrace of fine Georgian sandstone warehouses built more than 140 years ago, Salamanca Place forms a backdrop to Sullivan's Cove, and is now home to restaurants, art galleries, cafés and shops.

On Saturday, the couple went shopping in central Hobart, and then went to Salamanca Place again. It was market day and the area in front of the old warehouses was packed with tourists and locals. They browsed around the craft and general stalls for about two hours and shopped for fresh vegetables for Martin's mother, who was cooking them dinner at her home that night.

After dinner at Martin's mother's home, Petra and Martin went to the Cadillac Club, a city nightclub, but they left early. When they arrived home to Clare Street, Martin set the alarm for 6 a.m. He had something to do the next day, he told Petra.

He had seemed irritable for the last couple of days, but when they woke bright and early that Sunday his mood had lifted. The couple's usual routine was to go for a walk together on Sunday morning, before Petra drove back to her parents' home in the Huon Valley. But that Sunday, 28 April 1996, was different. Instead, Martin hurried Petra out of the house at about 8 a.m. He promised to see her again at eleven o'clock the next morning.

PART II
Black Sunday

CHAPTER 8
....

Something Wrong at the Seascape Guest House

The tourist season was nearing its end. It was late April and the number of visitors had begun to dwindle, but the Seascape guest house, on the Arthur Highway, about 2.5 kilometres north of the Port Arthur Historic Site, had four guests for breakfast on Sunday morning, 28 April. It was 8.30 a.m. A couple from Hobart had checked in the afternoon before, and were greeted with a cup of tea. The other guests were two women from Sydney, work colleagues, who had spotted Seascape as they drove past early on Saturday afternoon. When they returned later and checked in, the friendly owner had arranged a Port Arthur ghost tour for that evening.

At breakfast, Seascape owners Sally and David Martin

were their usual genial selves. It was David's seventy-second birthday. Despite their years, the Martins were an energetic pair, continuing a lifetime of hard work with great enthusiasm. Seven days a week they worked, but it didn't seem to faze either of them. For Sally, work was a way of life: she had been only nine years old when her mother died, and she had immediately begun helping her father run his Hobart butcher shop. Every afternoon after school she could be found behind the counter.

Since their wedding in the late 1940s, David had been a shipwright and a farmer. The couple had built and operated a general store in the riverside suburb of Bellerive for ten years before buying a small farm near Port Arthur.

Then, in the early 1980s, the Martins bought a rather neglected house in an idyllic setting beside the water near Port Arthur, and transformed it into Seascape, one of Tasmania's most charming guest houses. The leap into tourism had occurred at a time in their lives when most people contemplate retirement, but the Martins had no thoughts of taking things easy. Their pleasure was in meeting people and making them welcome.

The Martins's two sons were always around to help out. During their first years at Seascape, Glenn was just down the road, running the Port Arthur store, and Darren was a regular visitor. The Martins also retained their small farm near Port Arthur.

They'd been able to take only one major holiday together – a three-month tour along the east coast of Australia – but, for the Martins, Seascape brought the rest of the world to their door. They had scores of letters and cards sent by guests over the years.

The women from Sydney headed off early to continue their tour of the Tasman Peninsula, but the Hobart couple were in no hurry and stayed chatting to their hosts. When Sally went off to do some laundry, David invited them to have a look at another cottage on the property.

It was about 11.20 a.m. when the last guests finally prepared to drive off. As she always did, Sally came out to bid them farewell.

At 12.30 p.m., an elderly Victorian couple just completing a short fly–drive holiday to Tasmania were on their way from Port Arthur to the airport in the hope of being able to change their tickets for an earlier plane to Melbourne.

They had seen Seascape from the road as they drove to Port Arthur that morning and, like so many others, had fallen in love with what they saw. They had decided to call in on the drive back, and ask if they could inspect the property. If they came back to Tasmania, they thought, Seascape might be just the place at which to spend a night or two.

The couple drove off the highway, down the driveway and over the little bridge, and parked beside the house. There was another car near the front door, but they took little notice of it.

As they walked from their own car towards the front door, a young man with shoulder-length hair suddenly appeared from the doorway. There was something wrong, very wrong. The young man was agitated, excited, as his rapid hand movements clearly showed. His voice sounded strange, and he couldn't keep still. The woman became nervous, and wondered if he might be on drugs. Certainly he was behaving very strangely. All her instincts told her they should get away from him as soon as possible.

The woman's husband asked if they could have a look at one of the rooms, but the man refused, saying that his mother and father were out for ten minutes. Then he added that he couldn't show them around because his girlfriend was inside the house.

They turned and hurried to their car. Driving back to the highway, the woman looked back and saw the young man still standing at the door, staring after them.

CHAPTER 9

A Day for Settling "Scores"

Martin Bryant had four more calls to make on that Sunday afternoon as he drove out of the driveway at Seascape guest house. But first he drove down the Arthur Highway and turned left into Safety Cove Road towards Carnarvon Bay, where he had spent all his childhood holidays – the place where the other children had called him "silly Martin". He wanted to see again the shacks once owned by his family. And there were some neighbours he wanted to meet again – Maurice and Jillian Williams.

The drive down Safety Cove Road took him past its junction with Palmers Lookout Road. He also passed David and Sally Martin's farm – the farm he had always wanted to own, the farm they had refused to sell to him. Perched on a hill overlooking part of the Port Arthur Historic Site, it was as rustic and beautiful as ever.

Martin also knew the adjoining farm along Palmers

Lookout Road. It was owned by Roger and Marian Larner, whom he had known for most of his life. Like David and Sally Martin, and Maurice and Jillian Williams, the Larners had unwittingly earned his hatred.

The yellow Volvo cruised into Tasman Street and stopped. Bryant knocked on a door across the road from the Williams's place. There was nobody at home there or across the road at the Williams's. The Williamses were out, and were not due back from a holiday at their daughter's place until later in the day.

Back at the Larners's farm, Marian and Roger had finished lunch some time before. They had broken their long-established routine of having lunch at one o'clock in their farmhouse beside the Palmers Lookout Road. Their four-year-old grandson was with them that day. When he began to get fractious and hungry, they had decided to eat lunch an hour earlier than usual, and had sat down around midday.

It was exactly one o'clock when Roger Larner walked out the back door, climbed into his ute and drove one hundred metres down the road to his stockyards. As he pulled up, a yellow Volvo with a surfboard on the roof approached with the lights flashing and the horn tooting. It stopped, and the driver got out and approached.

At first Roger Larner didn't recognise Martin Bryant. The Martin Bryant he and his wife had known for eighteen years, and had last seen two years before, didn't have shoulder-length blond hair.

"Who is it?" asked Roger.

"It's Martin. How's the health?"

"Fine," replied the farmer. "Yourself?"

"Oh, mine's pretty good," said Martin. "I don't smoke any more and I don't drink much."

It was just polite chit-chat beside a country road between a couple of people who had lost touch with each other for a year or two. They talked for about ten minutes. Bryant said he was down on the Tasman Peninsula for some surfing, and also hoped to buy some cattle. He wanted a couple of heifers and a bull.

Roger knew the Copping farm had been sold, so asked Bryant where he was going to run the cattle.

"Oh, I've bought a farm up past New Norfolk called Frog Lodge. I would have liked to have bought the Martins's farm next door to you, but of course they wouldn't sell." Bryant added that he had just been down the road to see the old family shack at Carnarvon Bay and found that a large new house had been built on the site.

It was a comfortable conversation. Roger Larner felt that it was the most normal he had ever seen Martin Bryant: he was calm, coherent, asking sensible questions and making sensible responses. It was a pleasant change from the conduct they and the other locals had grown used to. Bryant was about ten when his parents first obtained a holiday shack nearby and, as a teenager, he and his sister, Lindy, were taught to ride on the farm by Marian Larner. Their mother, Carleen, was a good horsewoman and a familiar sight around Port Arthur.

In those days, the Port Arthur Historic Site was maintained by the Department of Parks and Wildlife, and the locals and visitors alike had open access. Eventually, Carleen and her children had their own horses which were agisted on the Larners's farm.

It had been obvious from the outset that Martin Bryant was different from other children. The Larners always felt that he was not quite a normal child, but not bad enough to be in an institution. He wouldn't associate with other children, and was always on his own. "Not quite the full shilling" was the expression the locals would use to sum him up.

During the riding lessons he sometimes fitted the bridle back to front, and when this was pointed out to him he would reply that it worked all right and the horse didn't mind.

Martin was about sixteen when Roger Larner discovered that thirty or forty trees on a forested part of his farm had been cut down, and that the teenager was to blame. The farmer's first concern was that the boy could have been killed, as some of the trees were quite substantial, and his felling technique had been like a woodpecker, circling the trees with an axe.

There was no question of confronting the kid about the matter. Like many of their neighbours, the Larners knew that it was best not to antagonise Martin but to keep him on an even keel. Instead, Roger told Martin's mother and asked her to speak to her son. Roger had added that, seeing the boy had so much energy, he might like a job mowing the lawns around the farmhouse. The Bryants had agreed, and it had been working out quite well until Martin stripped a lemon tree and threw the lemons into a paddock. Then, on another occasion, he pulled carrots from the ground and placed them on all the fence posts. Martin Bryant got the sack, but the decision was communicated to his mother.

Martin had lost interest in horse riding and switched to diving and fishing with his father. The Larners gradually lost contact. And then their paths crossed again. It was a

Tuesday, in August 1993, and Marian Larner was attending Hobart's Calvary Hospital for a check-up. She had just walked out of the hospital car park on her way into the hospital when she met Martin. She didn't think that was strange, because she knew his parents lived next door to the hospital.

Martin grabbed Marian by the shoulders. "Oh, Marian, it's so exciting. So exciting."

"What are you talking about, Martin?" she asked him.

"Dad's at the bottom of the dam. You'll hear all about it soon. You'll read all about it."

Marian thought Martin was talking nonsense, as he often did. In any case, she was preoccupied with her medical appointment.

But he wouldn't let her go. "Come with me. Come and have a cup of tea. Let me make you a cup of tea. Come home."

Marian refused, saying she had an appointment.

The following Thursday, Marian Larner was called by the hospital and told she was needed back there on Friday. The same day, the Larners heard that Martin's father, Maurice, was missing on the Copping farm.

He was outside the hospital again when she arrived there on the Friday, and insisted she come home with him. "I'm sorry to hear about your father," she said and then explained to him that she didn't want to go to his home, that again she had an appointment.

A few weeks later Marian Larner began to receive phone calls at night from Bryant. The calls were always made when she was alone. Again, the invitation was to come and have cups of tea – this time at the farm at Copping, midway between Hobart and Port Arthur.

"I know you're at home by yourself because Roger has gone past," Bryant would say. He became increasingly insistent, offering to come over and pick her up.

Marian started to worry. It was annoying behaviour and odd, and she was aware that she was rejecting him. Bryant had never liked being refused anything by anybody. Nor did she have any way of knowing whether he was phoning from Hobart or Copping, or from a nearby phone box. Added to that she was starting to think again about the excited claim: "Dad's at the bottom of the dam." Had it just been a piece of nonsense, or had he known something?

She decided to phone the local policeman, who came around the following day and took a statement. She didn't really want to complain, she said, but she felt uneasy. The officer said they would have a talk to Martin and warn him off, and to let him know if there was any further bother. But Marian Larner received no further calls.

Apart from a fleeting glimpse of Bryant and his mother at Hobart airport a couple of years ago, that was the last the Larners had seen or heard of Bryant. Until now.

"Is your missus around?" Martin Bryant asked Roger Larner, after they had been chatting for about ten minutes.

Yes, Larner replied, she was in the house doing the washing up.

"Would it be all right if I go up and see her?"

"Guess so," said Roger, but then added that he would come with him. And perhaps Bryant would like to see some heifers that were for sale.

Suddenly Martin changed his mind. No, he had to go to Nubeena. He would come back later in the afternoon, if that was all right. Would the Larners be home then?

Most likely, said Roger, and went about doing chores while Bryant drove back down the road. It was the last Roger saw of him.

He put the ute away in the shed. Then, just as he walked through the garden gate, he heard shooting. But that wasn't unusual. Gunshots could often be heard around the peninsula.

Inside the house, Marian went hot and cold when she heard Bryant had been around and that he was planning to return. She wasn't sure she wanted to talk to him. Did he know she had complained to the police? He must, she thought. Would he ask her about it? She decided to take the dogs for a long walk, so that she wouldn't be around when he returned.

CHAPTER 10

"Everyone Thought it was a Re-enactment..."

The honeymooners from Queensland missed the turn off the highway into the Port Arthur Historic Site and had to continue on to a T-junction a few hundred metres further on before they could turn around and backtrack. As they pulled over to prepare to turn, James and Joanne Dutton noticed a yellow Volvo with a surfboard on top driving up the side road towards them and the highway.

The Volvo, with a lone occupant, passed them and headed towards Port Arthur, and a minute or two later they noticed the same car at the toll booth.

After studying the information board and site map near the booth, the Duttons drove down to the parking area, bought some tickets for the Isle of the Dead tour at 3 p.m., and waited for the free 1.30 p.m. guided walking tour.

A walking tour is a highlight of any visit to the Port Arthur Historic Site, not least because the guides are well trained and full of information mixed with grim and amusing anecdotes about daily life in the Port Arthur of 150 years ago.

Tourists had begun gathering early for the 1.30 walking tour that Sunday, and the numbers waiting outside the information office had swelled to seventy or eighty.

As they stood amidst the crowd, waiting for their guide to appear, the Duttons heard a noise. A series of loud shots rang out. Startled, they looked towards the café and saw a man fall against a window. It must be a re-enactment, some staged entertainment for the tourists, they agreed. People began to mill around, trying to look into the café.

In the car park, the site's security officer, Ian Kingston, heard the loud banging coming from the Broad Arrow Café. He had no idea what it was: perhaps it was a gas explosion from the kitchen, or maybe the gas cookers themselves had exploded. What threw him was the sight of dust coming out of the wall at the end of the building.

Kingston was 30 metres from the Broad Arrow. He ran to the front door. It was open, and two bodies were on the floor. He hardly registered them. Kingston was puzzled by the dust and looked at the ceiling in search of some structural damage. As he did so, there was more banging and his ears began to ring. He looked up.

A man was directly in front, about 4 to 6 metres away, with his back to him. The man held a gun at hip height, and was shooting people as they sat at the tables. He appeared to be in no hurry: he was almost casual as he chose his victims, shooting some from a range of no more than a metre.

Unarmed and realising there was no chance of rushing the gunman and overpowering him, Kingston shouted a warning to staff member Colleen Parker, who was standing at the servery. He saw twelve people shot before he escaped back out through the door and began trying desperately to get people to flee the area.

Brigid Cook, supervisor of the Broad Arrow's kitchen, had also been on her way to investigate the crackling noise. It sounded like something electrical: perhaps the coffee machine or the bain marie had shorted out. Suddenly Colleen Parker ran into the kitchen from the serving counter.

"Don't go out there! Don't go out there!" she was shouting.

Brigid saw by Colleen's expression that something awful was happening. She fled to the car park, waving people back from the Broad Arrow and telling them to take cover. Even as she and Ian Kingston shouted warnings, tourists continued to walk towards the café, thinking that the shots were part of a re-enactment. They strolled, seemingly quite unconcerned, as the firing continued.

CHAPTER 11

The Broad Arrow Café

Sitting in the Broad Arrow Café with his girlfriend, Kate Scott, and friend Caroline Villiers, Mick Sargent, the keen drag racer, who had come to Tasmania to be best man at his mate's wedding, had surveyed the crowd, half daydreaming, as he ate a pile of potato wedges. Young and old, most were probably tourists like himself, Mick thought distractedly.

Then he had noticed a young blond man move to a table. It was the multi-coloured Prince sports bag that first caught Mick Sargent's eye. It looked heavy, not the kind of thing a person would want to lug around a tourist attraction, particularly when carrying a video camera in the other hand. The smart thing to do would have been to leave it in the car or tour coach.

He watched as the man put the bag on a table. The man suddenly realised he was being watched, and the two held eye contact for about fifteen seconds. Something wasn't right, Mick felt. It seemed like the fellow was hassling him, that he didn't like the look of him. So Mick held his stare to show that he wasn't scared.

The duel was interrupted when Kate asked Mick a question. He turned to answer her. When Mick looked back to check if he was still being hassled, the man was standing beside the table where he'd placed his bag and was looking towards an Asian couple. He was starting to unzip the bag. Mick turned away again and continued talking to Kate and Caroline.

Five or ten seconds later there was a deafening sound. It was a gunshot. Mick looked up just as the man with the bag shot the Asian woman with a gun. She flew back up against the window. Then he swung the gun around and aimed it straight at Mick's head from about 4 metres away. Mick dived for the floor as the killer pulled the trigger. The bullet grazed the top of his head, splitting the skin. Mick heard another shot fired immediately after. Kate hit the floor about half a metre away.

Mick lay there, thinking he'd been shot through the head. He could feel blood running down both sides of his head and neck, and a burning sensation. "This is it. I'm going to die and it's going to take a few seconds to happen," he thought. He crawled over to Kate. She'd been shot in the head. He knew she was dead. "Now we can die together," he thought, and he waited for everything to go black. Then it hit him. He wasn't dying. Several seconds had passed and he was still conscious.

As he lay there beside Kate the firing continued. The noise was deafening – boom, boom, boom – and he struggled to regain his senses, to somehow survive.

Convinced that the gunman would return to finish off anyone he had wounded or missed, Mick hid his head beneath Kate's arm and tried to remain still. By listening to the shots, he could work out when the gunman was firing towards the area they were in and when he had the gun pointing away. He moved his head and stole a quick glance. The killer flashed past and did a kind of pirouette as he swung around and started shooting people on the other side of the room. He had the gun up in the air and would spin with it in that position, then point it down to shoot. Bang, bang, up in the air, spin back around. He was like some crazed Rambo.

The gunman was very, very quick and seemed to be out for the maximum kill. Mick put his head down again. There was a window nearby, and he toyed with the idea of hurling a chair through it and diving out, but the risk of alerting the gunman was too great. In any case, he had seen people jump through windows and receive horrific injuries.

John Riviere was at the servery when he had heard two shots and the sound of glass breaking. The Asian couple were slumped in their seats and the gunman was laughing as he continued to shoot people. John looked towards the table where he had been sitting with Caroline, Mick and Kate and heard Mick saying to him: "Keep down, keep down." John hid behind the counter and then, when the gunman's back was turned, escaped through the side entrance.

Meanwhile, Mick saw Caroline Villiers sitting on the floor. At first he thought that she, too, had been shot. She was shaking and crying and beginning to panic, but she was unharmed. Worried she might attempt to make a run for it and be shot dead, he signalled with his hands for her to crawl over to him. She was only about 3 metres away.

Mick grabbed her head, put his arm around her, and held her down beside him.

Caroline was distraught. "I've got to get out of here; I've got to get out of here."

Mick tried to calm her and told her not to move, that they would be fine. He noticed that the shots were becoming a lot quieter and that the gunman was moving away, outside the café.

Mick decided they should take their chance, and grabbed Caroline by the hand. They ran out the side door along to a high retaining wall, where he could see others scrambling up. Mick pushed her up and over the top, and told her to run. He then returned to the café to be with Kate.

Outside, the shooting had stopped. The killer was reloading. Mick lay down beside Kate and put his hand on the middle of her back, but he couldn't feel her heart beating. It was a kind of relief: no-one would want to be alive with such a horrendous injury, he thought.

He heard somebody scream – it was a male voice – and realised there were other people the gunman had missed. Aware that there were wounded in the café, he found a phone just inside the door and dialled 000.

"Can I help you?" the operator inquired.

"Police, ambulance, the lot!" Mick shouted.

"Where to?"

But Mick was in shock and couldn't, for the life of him, remember where he was. "Where are we?" he called to anyone who might listen.

"Port Arthur," came the answer from some people who had just walked into the café.

"Port Arthur, Port Arthur," he yelled down the phone. "Port Arthur. Bring everything you've got!"

Mick returned to Kate's side. Gradually he became aware of others attending to the wounded. Someone was running errands, bringing tea towels to be used as bandages. He looked around to see if there was anybody he could help. It was then he realised the magnitude of the shootings. It was a disaster area, with bodies everywhere. They'd all been shot out of their chairs.

A woman sat amidst a sea of bodies, about four or five people. They were all her friends. Mick walked over and asked if she was okay.

She said: "I'm fine, but my husband is dead."

Mick could see that the man had suffered a fatal head wound. "Yes, I know that. My girlfriend is dead as well. Is there anything I can do to help you?"

When she again said she was fine, Mick told her that, if she needed him, he would be with Kate, who was about 5 metres away.

Mick again returned to Kate. He began to talk to her, saying comforting things. "It's all right, Kate, you're going to a very nice place. You will like it there."

He looked up to see the woman he had spoken to earlier, standing quietly, just looking at him. It was obvious she had heard him talking but didn't want to intrude. He stood up and put his arms around her and held her, telling her they had to be strong. There must be a reason why we have survived, he said. The woman thanked him and returned to her husband's side.

Mick began to move around the Broad Arrow covering some of the dead with tea towels, and also covering some of the blood and other matter on the tables. But it got to be too much for him. He went back to Kate and said to the dead woman, "I've got to go. I can't handle this any longer. This is spinning me right out."

He ran out to the toilets, and cleaned some of the blood from himself. He wanted to make himself look a bit respectable.

CHAPTER 12

Like Rabbits in a Trap

It will never be known how many lives were saved by the actions of site security manager, Ian Kingston, kitchen supervisor, Brigid Cook, and other workers and visitors, including New South Wales police officer Justin Noble, as they shepherded hundreds of people to safety.

Ian Kingston had joined Port Arthur less than a year before. As manager of the Tasman Peninsula's State Emergency Service (SES) unit, which he helped establish in 1984, he came equipped with what were to prove invaluable qualifications. The SES unit's twenty members are trained in first aid and search and rescue techniques. Together with the volunteer fire brigades and the volunteer ambulance officers, they are the Tasman community's mini-army of self-help. In all there are a total of 150 volunteers – in a district with a permanent population of only 2000.

Kingston's struggle to disperse the crowds up towards the old church and relative safety had proved only partly successful, and people continued to stream across the site towards the café. It was wall to wall people trying to get in to see the action of what they thought must be a re-enactment.

Kingston had reached the intersection of Tarleton Street and Jetty Road when he looked back and saw the gunman emerge from the Broad Arrow. The man fired a couple of shots across the site, then went to the boot of his car, the yellow Volvo, and got out another magazine. He let another four or more shots go, across towards the Commandant's House, then walked on to one of the buses.

Kingston didn't see what had happened on the buses; he was too involved in moving others to safety. When the man drove from the site seven or eight minutes later, Kingston had reached the Parsonage, about 150 metres away up on the hill behind the old church.

He phoned the police. His emergency service training taking over, he warned police not to let ambulance teams onto the site until it was known whether or not the gunman was still running rampant. Kingston also phoned the toll booth to warn Aileen Kingston of what was happening. She told him she had already been warned. While Kingston talked, Aileen could hear shooting just down the road, and the site security manager realised the gunman had left the café area. Aileen Kingston locked herself in the toll booth and lay on the floor.

Other Port Arthur staff herded visitors into the various cottages to move them out of the line of fire. Kingston went back to manage the scene outside the Broad Arrow. People were already there, giving first aid to the wounded. But there were others outside with pieces missing out of their legs, out of their necks. They were still walking around in shock.

There were bodies in the café and on the buses. It was chaotic, so Kingston climbed onto the roof of a car in the car park and shouted at the crowd, to try to get their attention. "The gunman has gone. Everyone try to stay calm! You're all safe now. If anyone needs urgent medical attention, please come and inform us immediately!"

Brigid Cook, the kitchen supervisor in the café, had been hiding with others beside some of the tour buses. "There he is!" somebody suddenly shouted. The gunman was about a bus-and-half-length away. The care that he took of himself struck her. He appeared to be having a fine time, a very exciting time, but he made sure there was no way he could be snuck up on.

Suddenly he spotted Brigid. He raised the gun to his eye and pointed it at her. She couldn't see his face. She knew she was a good target in her white top and black pants. As the gun fired, Brigid jumped sideways. It may have saved her life, but the bullet struck her in the thigh.

Using the first aid she had been taught when she first joined the Port Arthur staff, Brigid staunched the flow of blood with her apron. Then the gunman left, and a deathly quiet descended. No-one dared make a noise, in case he came back.

But Brigid remained calm. A little later, she was able to tell others where to find clean tea towels in the Broad Arrow to use as first aid on some of the wounded. There were also drinks and food which could be distributed.

Wendy Scurr, who worked in the information office, had overseen the first-aid training at Port Arthur. From the glass-fronted office, only metres from the gunman, she phoned a message to alert police to what was happening, as shots continued to ring out from the Broad Arrow. Wendy knew that the isolation of the Tasman Peninsula meant that help would take time to arrive. She was also worried that she wouldn't be believed by the operator at police headquarters. Who, after all, could possibly believe what was happening around her?

"There's slaughter going on! People being killed everywhere! For God's sake, get help!" She gave them her name and was asked for a phone number where she could be contacted. She said she wouldn't be there.

After getting her call through, Wendy and another information officer, Sue Burgess, took cover in the bush immediately behind the buildings. Other staff members were hiding there, as well as Steven Howard, an information officer who earlier had been helping to man the toll booth.

Wendy heard on a two-way radio that the gunman had left his car and was on foot. Everyone was terrified: would he come back? They were all so vulnerable, like rabbits in a trap.

But they went down into the café to help the victims, nevertheless. Little could be done for some of them. Among the dead were Sue Burgess's seventeen-year-old daughter, Nicole, and Steven Howard's wife, Elizabeth. Despite their shock and grief, Burgess and Howard stayed to assist Wendy Scurr and others with the wounded.

Wendy had no idea how long they worked in the café. Time seemed to have stopped.

CHAPTER 13

Murder on the Road

When Brigid Cook had run out of the Broad Arrow Café, waving her arms and shouting for people to run for cover, James and Joanne Dutton, the honeymooners from Queensland who were lined up to join the 1.30 walking tour, had started to head for the toll booth exit. It was several hundred metres away. James looked back over his shoulder and saw a man armed with a gun emerge from the café and move into and around the coaches parked nearby.

The Duttons ran toward the exit, staying close to the trees bordering the road. They could see other people running across the grass towards the Government Gardens and the ruined church.

As they climbed the hill, random shots continued. A woman stood nearby, with two little girls. It was Nanette Mikac with her two daughters, Alannah, aged six, and Madeline, aged three.

Nanette Mikac, a ghost tour guide at Port Arthur, had brought her little girls to have a picnic lunch in the grounds. Nanette's husband, Walter, was the local pharmacist. That Sunday he was at the Tasman Golf Club, playing a round with some friends.

The Mikacs had arrived from Melbourne two years before to establish the Tasman Pharmacy at Nubeena – the first on the Tasman Peninsula. The business, and their arrival, were warmly welcomed by the community, and they had been quickly accepted.

The lack of a pharmacy had been identified as one of the major problems for the district, and a report on a meeting discussing the issue was published in the local newspaper. Nanette Mikac's parents had retired to White Beach, near Nubeena, and they told their son-in-law about the opportunity to set up on the peninsula. Walter had come down to investigate and had asked Neil Noye, the Mayor of Tasman, if suitable premises might be available. Noye suggested the former Church of Christ building in the main street. And so the Mikacs had come to Nubeena to live.

On the way up Jetty Road towards the exit, another fleeing couple – John and Caroline Boskovic – heard Nanette Mikac trying to comfort Alannah, who was running along beside her. "We're safe now, pumpkin," the Boskovics heard Mrs Mikac say.

Then the yellow Volvo drew up. Mrs Mikac, no doubt thinking it offered escape, turned towards the car.

James Dutton had shouted "Run" as he heard the car approaching and, as he looked back, he recognised the vehicle as the one he and Joanne had seen at the turnoff.

The gunman got out of the car, put his hand on Mrs Mikac's shoulder and ordered her three times to kneel.

She pleaded with him: "Please, don't hurt my babies." Instead, the man shot Nanette Mikac dead, then killed three-year-old Madeline. Terrified, Alannah hid behind a nearby tree. Dutton tried, unsuccessfully, to grab her as he and his wife ran past to seek shelter in the scrub.

In the most callous moment of his entire rampage, the gunman fired two shots at Alannah, missed, then walked towards her and pressed the rifle barrel to her neck before firing.

The Duttons heard more shots as they ran further into the scrub and took cover.

Up the road at the toll booth, a couple in a car were just about to drive in. June Edward and her husband, Keith, both in their sixties, were visitors from Port Macquarie in New South Wales. As they started to move forward, June suddenly noticed a man some distance down the road point a rifle at a woman and child, who then fell to the ground. Quickly the Edwards reversed out. They stopped to pick up two terrified New Zealanders, Thomas and Debra Buckley, from Mosgiel. They, too, had seen the shootings.

The Buckleys had just paid their entrance fee when they heard a warning and began to reverse out. They were following a BMW and had stopped behind it at the toll booth. Behind them they saw the gunman, who at first they thought was a woman, shoot a woman and a little girl. The Buckleys abandoned their car and ran towards the highway, where the Edwards picked them up. The four tourists then drove to the Port Arthur store and service station.

Keith Edward tried to warn other traffic and individuals. Looking up, he saw a BMW approaching from the direction of the Port Arthur site, with a gun pointed from the driver's side window.

Edward and the Buckleys escaped down the side of the shop. Sheltering inside the shop, Mrs Edward saw the gunman approach a car with two occupants and wave the gun at a man in the front seat, telling him to get out.

At gunpoint, the man was forced to the boot of the BMW. The gunman opened it, forced the man to climb in, and then slammed it shut. He then walked back to the other car, pointed the gun at the young woman inside and shot her. He then drove off in the BMW towards the Seascape guest house, 2.5 kilometres north along the Arthur Highway.

Behind him thirty-two people lay dead. The man still alive in the boot of the BMW was Glenn Pears. Glenn Pears's companion, now dead, was 28-year-old Zoe Hall.

CHAPTER 14

A Deathly Quiet

The morning service over, the newly ordained Church of Christ minister for the Tasman Peninsula, Glenn Cumbers, prepared to unwind for a few hours before his parishioners would begin to gather for the evening service at Nubeena.

Formerly from Wollongong, Cumbers had been a nurse before he decided on a change of vocation. He had arrived in Tasmania in January and had been ordained on 1 March.

Nubeena, with a population of 300, is the "capital" of the peninsula. It is less than a twenty-minute drive from Port Arthur. The Cumbers family had settled in well to the small community and enjoyed the lifestyle and the environment. That Sunday the autumn weather was delightful, with plenty of sunshine and a temperature that felt warmer than the ten or eleven degrees the forecast had promised.

The only people at all unhappy with the weather were the kids down at the Nubeena Sailing Club: there was barely a breath of breeze for their sailing races. The commodore of the club, Vietnam veteran and volunteer ambulance officer Gary Alexander, watched the kids set off in their boats, and then settled down with a cup of coffee to view their slow progress.

Autumn is the Tasman's best season. The locals like it because it signals the end of the summer crowds which swell the population to between four and five times the 2000 people who live there. In autumn, the peninsula becomes theirs once again.

Glenn Cumbers and his wife decided to do what many local residents do on a pleasant Sunday – drive down to the Port Arthur Historic Site for a picnic or lunch at the Broad Arrow Café.

Until relatively recently, the Port Arthur ruins had simply been part of the local stamping ground: the oval between the Broad Arrow Café and the ruins of the penitentiary was the locals' football ground and cricket ground, and the road to Nubeena went straight through the site.

Generations of summer holiday and weekend visitors from Hobart had pitched their tents in the grounds and spent a lazy summer fishing, bushwalking and socialising. Nowadays, the Port Arthur management authority issued free three-year passes to the locals so they could continue to use the area as they had always done.

On the way to or from the Broad Arrow, Glenn planned to return a video to the Port Arthur store near the toll booth. But the Cumbers changed their plans when Athol Bloomfield and his wife returned to the church to ask them to lunch. The Bloomfields lived in North Street, just down the road from the historic site.

The Cumbers and Bloomfields were nearing the end of their lunch when they heard shots. At first, Cumbers couldn't distinguish what the sounds were, because they were so loud, like mini explosions. They certainly sounded nothing like the .22s or the shotguns he was accustomed to hearing around the peninsula as locals went in search of rabbits, possums or feral cats.

The sounds were more like a blast, and they appeared to be coming from Port Arthur. Perhaps someone was trying to hold up the toll booth, they speculated. They phoned the site to find out what was going on. When the terrible situation was explained, Glenn Cumbers and Athol Bloomfield set off in the car for Port Arthur, to see if they could help.

Over at Nubeena, where the Cumbers's thirteen-year-old son was sailing, Gary Alexander's beeper sounded. Alexander was on call and had the ambulance with him. Ambulance headquarters in Hobart had also had a report of shooting at the historic site. By the time he had walked 20 metres to the vehicle, his co-volunteer Kaye Fox had arrived from her home a short distance away.

The sight and sound of the ambulance racing to Port Arthur that afternoon alerted many along the route that something serious had happened.

Cumbers and Bloomfield reached the toll booth a minute or two before the ambulance crew. There they found four bodies lying across the entrance. In the booth they found Aileen Kingston, the attendant, unharmed. Having locked herself in the booth, she had then hidden in the toilet when the gunman appeared.

A short distance further on, Cumbers found Nanette Mikac and her two daughters, Alannah, and Madeline. They were all dead. The children were members of his Sunday school. Almost overcome by shock, the minister knew immediately that none of his training as a nurse or ambulance officer could be of any use. All he could do was cover the three bodies.

Gary Alexander and Kaye Fox arrived and found a yellow Volvo with a surfboard on the roof abandoned near the toll booth. Beside it was the body of a man, and a short distance further down the entry road were those of two women and another man.

The Tasman Peninsula is a popular area for emergency services exercises. Alexander's first thought was that he had arrived at an exercise, because the bodies looked like mannequins laid out. "If it's a training set-up and they haven't told someone, gee I'll go crook," he thought to himself. But it became very real when he got out of the ambulance.

In the meantime, Athol Bloomfield had driven down into the site and seen the full horror of what had happened there. He hurried back to Cumbers, Alexander and Fox. "You better get down there quick!" he told them, then returned to the highway just beyond the toll booth to prevent anybody else entering. He realised that the crime site had to be preserved for police investigators.

Cumbers jumped into the ambulance with Alexander and Fox. Nothing had hit home by the time they reached the parking area: they still had no clear idea what had happened. Alexander parked the ambulance near the buses. He knew that it was the best spot for radio communication in a region where communications are notoriously difficult.

As they climbed out of the ambulance, people called out, giving them directions, and warning them that there was a gunman around. Unsure where the gunman was, the two men came across some of the dead and injured. Within minutes they had run out of bandages.

Nothing during his service in Vietnam or attending road accidents around the Tasman Peninsula had prepared Alexander for the sight near the Broad Arrow. There were dead and wounded scattered about, and hundreds of people milling around.

It was both shocking and eerie. There was none of the panic and hysteria that television programs often portray. Instead, it was quiet. People were just walking around in shock.

One man was wandering around helping others. He knew his wife had been shot dead, but he continued to assist the survivors. The fortitude and selflessness that several of the wounded displayed struck Alexander as he worked.

On a balcony, Cumbers and Alexander found a woman who had been shot in the thigh. "I'm all right," she told them. "Don't worry about me. Look after someone else." They found someone to stay with her, then went to help others.

But as bad as the scene was outside, it was no preparation for the disaster inside the café. The lump in Alexander's throat grew. It was immediately clear that most of the people were dead, but still he checked each individual. One man seemed to be just holding on. Alexander thought he could feel the faintest pulse — or was he just imagining it? A doctor came around. "I've got one here," Alexander called. As the doctor was checking the man, he changed colour and went cold.

Glenn Cumbers also went into the Broad Arrow to see if he could help. It was horrific; he saw dead people still sitting there hanging on to their cups. One poor man was holding his wife; they were just sitting at the table. He assisted a man with a severe neck wound before re-checking the bodies of the dead and covering them.

Then he went back outside. A woman walked up to him. "I know my husband is dead in there, but will you just go in and check again?" She watched as Cumbers entered the café. He returned to confirm that the man was dead.

The woman was very upset. "Would you please comfort this lady; she's just lost her husband," Cumbers said to another woman sitting nearby with two others.

"Our husbands are dead too," the woman looked up at him and said.

Cumbers could do nothing for them except to have all four sit together, link arms and comfort each other.

In all, he spent three hours at the site, and made a number of trips into the cafeteria at the request of relatives asking, as the first woman had, whether their dear ones were dead inside. On one occasion it meant searching through a jumble of bodies, all the while being conscious of the grief-stricken faces watching through the window.

CHAPTER 15

Operation Code Brown

It seems incongruous, insensitive even, to talk about luck being present on a day in which thirty-five people were murdered and eighteen others wounded. But a series of coincidences combined to ensure that the Royal Hobart Hospital managed the trauma so efficiently that other hospitals, including at least one in the United States, have since sought details of its disaster plan.

The first alert that something terrible had happened at Port Arthur came at 1.50 p.m., with a phone call from Tasmanian Ambulance Service paramedic Warwick Allen to Dr David Smart, the hospital's director of emergency medicine.

The ambulance paramedic and his colleague Peter Stride were about to fly to the scene by helicopter (a fourteen-minute flight). The message was that there were eight dead and six injured in a shooting incident. Smart began phoning other staff, including the nursing supervisor, to warn that the disaster plan, Code Brown, might need to be activated. The nursing shifts were due to change over at 2 p.m. Those clocking off were asked to stand by.

One of the other people Smart reached was Dr Rod Franks, the plan's co-ordinator. Code Brown had just had a major revision, the first for several years, and the final draft had landed on Franks's desk two days before. He and two emergency department nurses, Sharon Groves and Amanda Pregnell, had worked on the project for several months.

Luckily, the director of surgery, Dr Stephen Wilkinson, had been in the nearby Repatriation Hospital that morning, conducting an Early Management of Severe Trauma (EMST) course for twenty-five doctors from all over Australia. The course, presented by the Royal Australasian College of Surgeons in conjunction with hospital specialists, aims at improving capacity to respond to major emergencies. It is usually held in Tasmania only once a year, and one of the scenarios that morning had been a multiple shooting.

Most of the doctors who had taken part were still in Hobart. Wilkinson himself had just arrived home, and was back on duty within five minutes.

Franks, who was at a barbecue at Berriedale in the northern suburbs, had been on call that weekend, and was carrying a mobile phone. A count of six wounded was manageable with the hospital's normal staffing and preparation, but he asked Smart to call him when more details were received. In the meantime, he packed up and drove towards the hospital, figuring that, whatever the situation, he would probably be needed in the emergency department.

Shortly before 2 p.m., ambulance paramedic Warwick Allen again phoned Smart to report that the toll at Port Arthur was much higher, and that there were multiple scenes with perhaps fourteen dead and ten wounded. By that time, Franks was within two minutes of arrival at the hospital. Code Brown would be activated, he decided.

At ambulance headquarters, senior officers also felt that luck was on their side: eighteen volunteers were attending a training course, and some were able to bolster numbers at Port Arthur or help provide back-up in the Hobart area.

Franks had mixed feelings as he faced the first test of the plan. First, he had never been in charge of such a situation, and he worried whether the draft, that collection of papers, would stand up to the reality. Then there was the sense of absolute disbelief that such an event could happen in Tasmania. Franks wasn't alone in his disbelief: some medical and nursing people had thought the call-out was an exercise. Franks also held concerns for his wife's brother, who he knew was somewhere in the Port Arthur area kayaking.

But Code Brown worked to perfection and, by the time the first patient was delivered by helicopter onto the nearby Queens Domain, then shuttled by ambulance to emergency at 3.18 p.m., five fully equipped and staffed operating theatres were ready and the emergency department had some forty doctors on duty.

Dr Brian Walpole, a staff specialist who had been helping run the trauma course that morning, was also director of patient services. He had only just got home from the trauma course. He thought it was some kind of joke when he was phoned and told that there had been a shooting at Port Arthur. Much of the setting up of the emergency department had already been done when he arrived, and the next task was to clear the 25-bed ward 3A to receive the wounded.

Like most major public hospitals in Australia, the Royal runs at a very high capacity. Space had to be created to cope with the major incident. Admission of patients for elective surgery for the following week was cancelled. In all, some fifty operations were postponed.

Doctors checked wards to see which inpatients could be sent home early, or transferred to the Repatriation Hospital. By early evening about sixty beds were available. Private hospitals in Hobart were alerted to be ready to cover the Royal for the traditional Sunday emergencies of sporting injuries, minor road accident injuries and general illness.

For Jane Lennox, the clinical nurse consultant in ward 3A, Code Brown worked so well that it had been almost a relief when the first patient arrived. Everyone had been ready to go for some time, but they didn't really know what had happened except for what they had heard broadcast on television.

The preparations had taken less than eighty minutes. The last patients arrived at the hospital at 6.20 p.m.

The weapons used meant that many of the wounded had terrible injuries; in some cases masses of tissue had been blown away, and amputations were necessary.

By 8.30 p.m. all eighteen wounded had cleared the emergency department. For those working in emergency, it was over, but there was concern that the gunman was still free. The emergency staff knew from the ambulance officers that there was the potential for more people to be found wounded in the bush. Any time during the night, they could be required again.

Carleen Bryant with her newborn baby, Martin John, in 1967.

The young Martin Bryant with his father, Maurice, and baby sister, Lindy. In August 1993 the body of Maurice Bryant, aged sixty-four, was found in a farm dam at Copping. Despite there being rumours that the son could have been responsible for his father's death, the coroner's findings were that the retired waterside worker had died by drowning, consistent with suicide.

Helen Harvey (right) in fancy dress. This cheerful, eccentric heiress was to become Martin Bryant's friend and benefactor. They met in early 1987, when she hired him to do gardening and odd jobs.

The inner-suburban Hobart property at 30 Clare Street, New Town, was home to Helen Harvey and her twenty-six cats and twenty dogs. Following her death in a car accident in October 1992, Martin Bryant inherited her fortune. Martin – who at the age of eighteen had been assessed as an invalid pensioner, it having been determined there was no prospect of his ever being able to gain or maintain full-time employment – was now a wealthy young man. Although Helen Harvey's death was found to be accidental, she was said to have told neighbours that she always drove slowly because Bryant would sometimes yank suddenly at the steering wheel.

In the months leading up to the murders at Port Arthur, Martin Bryant — who had always been so careful about his appearance and conscious of good clothes — had begun to look scruffy. His hair was longer and he didn't dress smartly any more. Girlfriend Petra took this photograph of Bryant on 25 April 1996. Three days later, after hearing of the massacre at Port Arthur, she tore up the photograph.

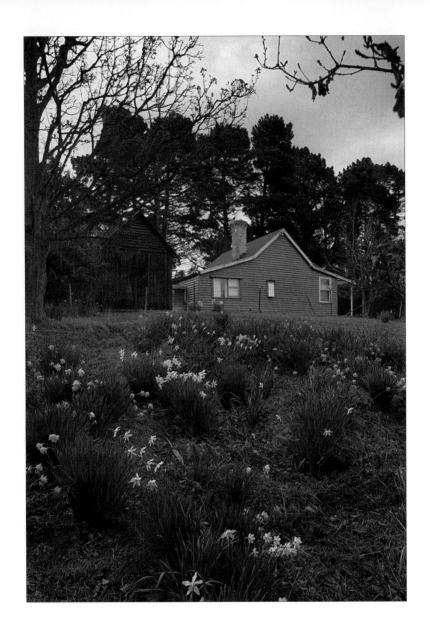

For at least fourteen years Martin Bryant had had a fixation about wanting to own Sally and David Martin's small farm on Palmers Lookout Road near Port Arthur. Even as a fifteen-year-old, he would pester the Martins about buying their farm. The couple were to be the first of Bryant's victims on 28 April 1996. (Photo: Leigh Winburn)

In the early 1980s Sally and David Martin bought a rather neglected house on Main Road, 2 kilometres north of the Port Arthur Post Office, and transformed it into one of Tasmania's most charming guest houses, Seascape. The leap into tourism had occurred at a time in their lives when most people contemplate retirement, but they had no thoughts of taking things easy. Their pleasure was in meeting people and making them welcome. Their guest house was to become the setting for their murder.

Sally and David Martin, about whom a Canadian woman said in a letter to the *Australian* newspaper: "Imagine two incredibly spry, grey-haired, inquisitive, talkative, trusting, grandparently hosts, who helpfully guided our stay in the area. Their kindness was immense . . . As I look at the picture of me and Sally standing on the front verandah of the quaint seashell pink cottage, I feel that the awful circumstances of their deaths should not go without a personal remembrance. May their families know that, half a world away, others cherish their memory and wish them eternal peace."

Roger and Marian Larner live next to the Martins's farm and have known Bryant since he was a boy. In 1993 Bryant accosted Marian Larner in the car park of Hobart's Calvary Hospital, where he told her: "Dad's at the bottom of the dam. You'll hear all about it soon. You'll read all about it." A few weeks later she began to receive unwelcome phone calls at night from Bryant. The Larners believe they could have been Bryant's victims on 28 April had they kept to their lunchtime routine. Bryant visited their farm just minutes before the shootings began. (Photo: Leigh Winburn)

A tourist's video camera captured this picture of Martin Bryant in the car park after he had shot dead twenty people in the Broad Arrow Café. The Colt AR15 semi-automatic assault rifle is being held close to his body.

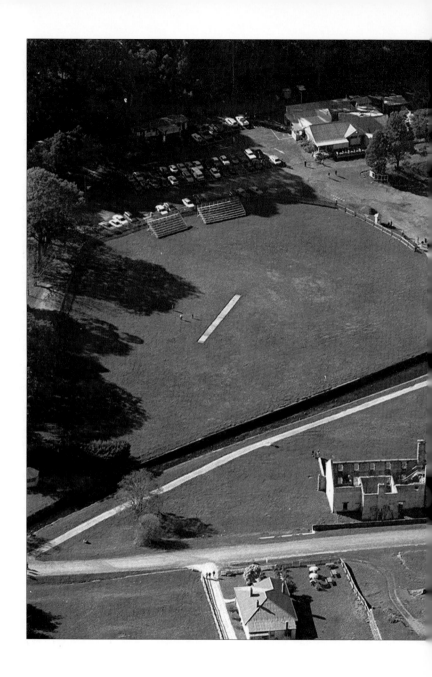

Port Arthur Historic Site from the air. In the middle foreground are the ruins of the Penitentiary. In the middle background is the Broad Arrow Café, where Bryant ate lunch before murdering twenty occupants of the

café. Tourists in the surrounding area, believing the gunshots to be part of a staged re-enactment, streamed towards the café.
(Photo: James Kerr)

Left, above: Kate Scott, aged twenty-one, with her boyfriend Mick Sargent, aged thirty, relaxing during their holiday in Tasmania. On the last day of their brief holiday they were determined to fit in some sightseeing before flying home to Western Australia. They set off for the famous convict ruins at Port Arthur, an easy ninety-minute drive south-east from Hobart. Later that day, at the Broad Arrow Café, the young woman Mick had planned to marry was shot dead.

Left, below: The Mikacs had arrived from Melbourne two years before to establish the Tasman Pharmacy at Nubeena – the first on the Tasman Peninsula. The business and their arrival were warmly welcomed by the community, and the family had been quickly accepted. On 28 April Walter Mikac lost his wife, Nanette, and daughters, Alannah, aged six, and Madeline, aged three. "It's like in an afternoon my whole life's just been erased," he said.

Above: Ian Kingston, site security manager. It will never be known how many lives were saved by the actions of Ian Kingston and Brigid Cook, kitchen supervisor, as well as other workers and visitors, as they shepherded hundreds of people to safety. (Photo: Fred Kohl)

Above: Police cordon off the Broad Arrow Café. (Photo: Leigh Winburn)
Right: By 8.30 p.m. on 28 April all the wounded from the Port Arthur Historic Site had been transported to Hobart by helicopters, ambulances and buses. Here, an ambulance officer attends to Brigid Cook, supervisor of the Broad Arrow's kitchen. A brave woman, she had fled from the kitchen to the car park to wave people back from the café and tell them to take cover. She was spotted by Bryant as she hid beside some tour buses. He raised his rifle and took aim. She jumped sideways as he fired, and received a bullet in the thigh. (Photo: Kim Eiszele)

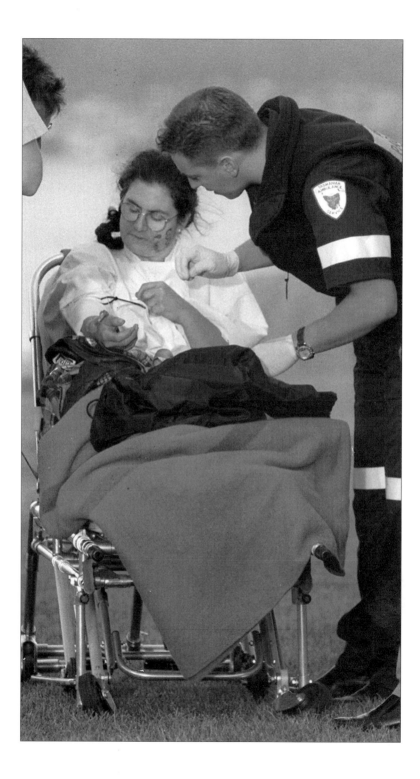

Members of the Special Operations Group being briefed before taking up their positions outside the Seascape guest house. At first, no-one knew whether the man who answered the telephone at the guest house and called himself "Jamie" was the same person responsible for the carnage at Port Arthur, nor if there was more than one gunman. (Photo: Barry Winburn)

Members of the Special Operations Group race across the Tasman Highway to take up their positions outside the Seascape guest house. Their task would be difficult: the guest house was set in the middle of a large paddock, and from the windows Bryant had a clear 360-degree view, preventing the Special Operations Group marksmen getting closer than 150 metres. (Photo: Robin Lane)

Above: Fire-fighters inspect the smouldering wreck of the Seascape guest house. On the morning of 29 April, Bryant set the guest house alight before running from the building with his clothing on fire. By 8.37 a.m. the siege was over and Bryant was bound and handcuffed. (Photo: Leigh Winburn)

Left, above: Sergeant Terry McCarthy, who led the team of police negotiators. Backed by other team members, plus a Hobart psychiatrist, Ian Sale, and the police psychologist Mike Ryan, McCarthy had had six separate conversations with the man who called himself "Jamie". (Photo: Leigh Winburn)

Left, below: Superintendent Bob Fielding briefing the media. Fielding was the forward commander at the Seascape siege in the early hours of 29 April and had the unenviable task of having to decide what to do about the hostages and whether to order the Special Operations Group to attack. Given the power of the weapons Bryant was using, a full-on assault on Seascape would have meant sending several police to their deaths. (Photo: Robin Lane)

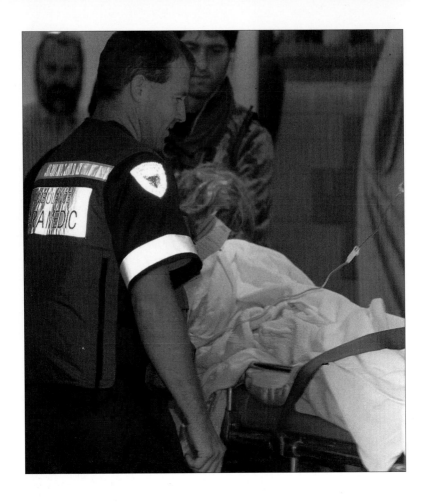

Martin Bryant arrives at the Emergency entrance to the Royal Hobart Hospital with serious burns to his back and buttocks. A Special Operations Group police officer watches as paramedic Peter Stride attends to Bryant's stretcher. Six days later, he was transferred from the burns unit to Risdon Prison. (Photo: Fred Kohl)

Two of Bryant's weapons. The Colt AR15 semi-automatic assault rifle (top) is no more than a metre in length; even with a full magazine (thirty rounds of .223 calibre) it weighs less than 4 kilograms. The FN FAL semi-automatic rifle (bottom) is a little over a metre in length; with a full magazine (twenty rounds of .308 calibre) it weighs less than 4 kilograms. He also had a loaded twelve-gauge shotgun with a ten-round detachable box magazine.

After the state service on 1 May at Saint David's Cathedral, Hobart, Prime Minister John Howard stopped on the steps of the cathedral to speak with Dr Bryan Walpole of the Royal Hobart Hospital's Department of Emergency Services Medicine. After the tragic events at Port Arthur, the Prime Minister – whose Liberal government had come into power on 2 March – promised to ensure there would be tighter gun control. He later announced there would be a ban on automatic and semi-automatic weapons and a buy-back scheme funded by Canberra – a message that drew a hostile reception from the gun lobby. (Photo: Leigh Winburn)

Outside the cathedral, Bronwyn Clifford of Cygnet in southern Tasmania holds a single rose as she and her friend observe the minute's silence during the service. Loudspeakers carried the service to the crowd of mourners outside the cathedral. In his address the Anglican Bishop of Tasmania, the Right Reverend Phillip Newell, said: "The destruction of beautiful lives and the wastefulness of it all have immersed us in a sorrow we have never known before." (Photo: Leigh Winburn)

Friends and family of the dead and wounded stand behind thirty-five white wooden crosses during the public memorial service held at the Port Arthur Historic Site on 19 May. Some 6000 people gathered for the service. Neil Noye, the Tasman Peninsula's civil leader, addressed the assembly. "We had never thought our beautiful peninsula would be the scene for such a

horrific crime against humanity. Our confidence in the old solid values of life, held by people of goodwill everywhere, was badly shaken. How could we ever recover, we asked ourselves . . . But today, less than a month on, we gather here as a community bound together by a common belief in the collective goodness of humanity." (Photo: Leigh Winburn)

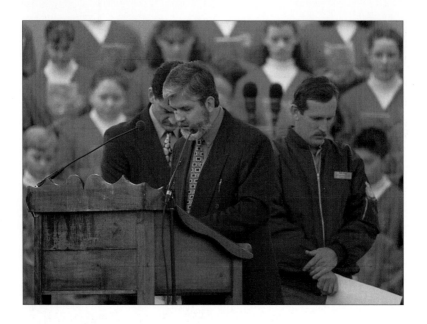

Glenn Cumbers, the minister from the Tasman Peninsula's Church of Christ at the nearby town of Nubeena, offers prayers for those killed and injured. He was a new minister – having moved to Tasmania in January and having been ordained in March – when he and his wife decided to take advantage of the pleasant weather of 28 April and have lunch with friends who lived near the Port Arthur Historic Site. Cumbers spent three hours at the site, comforting the relatives of the dead and using his earlier training as a nurse and ambulance officer. Weeks after the massacre, he was still struggling to come to terms with what he had experienced and the challenges it presented to his faith. The images of what he had seen recurred again and again, and it would be months before he was able to sleep properly. "I saw what he [Martin Bryant] did that day, and it makes me angry . . . that he was able to do it because he was able to get those weapons." (Photo: Leigh Winburn)

During the public memorial service held at the Port Arthur Historic Site for the thirty-five people slain by Martin Bryant, thirty-five white pigeons were freed to circle the site. The Premier of Tasmania, Tony Rundle, told the crowd that there was no sense or reason for the wickedness that had occurred three weeks before. "Yet even on that blackest day there were great shafts of light. Wickedness passes – but courage, strength in adversity, and hope for the future are with us forever. In just twelve weeks the daffodils will bloom, and blossom will burst forth from the trees." (Photo: Tony Palmer)

Superintendent Jack Johnston briefs the media. He headed the special taskforce investigating the shooting of each of the thirty-five people killed, and of those who were wounded. There were six crime scenes over a distance of more than 2 kilometres, and hundreds of people were caught up in the events. Over the next sixteen weeks the taskforce collected more than 840 statements throughout Australia. Through Interpol they conducted inquiries in Sweden, South Africa, the United States, Singapore, New Zealand and Malaysia. He and his team designed an innovative computer program linking hundreds of statements to 1200 photographs, plus exhibits, coronial material, maps, diagrams and video footage. An intricate cross-referencing system enabled the taskforce to reveal any gaps in the investigations. (Photo: Leigh Winburn)

Walter Mikac joined the National Coalition for Gun Control and took his message to rallies in Hobart, Melbourne and Sydney. On 28 July, in Sydney, 3000 people gathered at the Domain to hear him urge Australians to keep up pressure for the promised gun reforms. "As you all know, three months ago to this day I lost the entire reason for my existence," he said. (Photo: Fred Kohl)

An artist's impression of Martin Bryant in court. On 30 September 1996 he stunned the nation by pleading not guilty to seventy-two charges, including thirty-five charges of murder, twenty charges of attempted murder, eight charges of wounding, five charges of aggravated assault and three charges of causing grievous bodily harm. He later changed his plea to guilty.

CHAPTER 16

A Man Called "Jamie"

Sergeant Brett Smith and his team of seven were midway through their shift in the police radio room in Hobart when an anonymous caller to the 000 line reported that there was a person discharging a firearm at Port Arthur. It was 1.32 p.m. on Sunday, 28 April, and for a minute or two the message caused no real alarm or excitement. There were always recreational shooters out and about in the bush that covers much of the Tasman Peninsula.

"You had better take a look at this," the operator who handled the call alerted Brett Smith. Then the lines went berserk: someone had been shot, twelve people had been shot, the gunman was on the loose. The first detailed report came from Wendy Scurr, the information officer and volunteer ambulance member at the Port Arthur Historic Site.

At 1.35 p.m., Ian Kingston, the Port Arthur security officer and chief of the peninsula's SES unit, reported that seven people had been shot dead.

Another caller was Jim Laycock, who had once owned the Broad Arrow Café. Laycock owned the Kodak photo shop on the highway just outside the site entrance. He was there with his son-in-law when they heard shots. Laycock's son-in-law had served in the Greek army and recognised the shots as coming from a military style weapon.

The two men had walked outside the shop and could see activity around the toll booth. Then suddenly a red car came towards them like a bat out of hell.

The driver pulled up in front of the shop. "Quick! Ring the police. There's a maniac there. He's gone mad! He's shooting people!"

The car had sped off across the road. Laycock reported that he could see bodies beside a car near the toll booth.

Back in the radio room in Hobart, the atmosphere was unreal. The operators struggled to come to terms with what they were hearing. They yelled to each other across the room as more and more calls were received. By the end of that day the Hobart radio room would have received 4500 calls, more than six times the usual number.

The police officer nearest to Port Arthur was at Saltwater River, about twenty-five minutes away on the other side of the peninsula. Sergeant Smith dispatched units from Bellerive on Hobart's eastern shore, then contacted Luppo Prins, one of the two assistant commissioners. While trying to collate all the incoming information and to get police to the scene, Smith also activated the major incident room.

The pressure on the sergeant and the operators was not due simply to the necessity to organise a quick police response. While the race was on to contact off-duty police officers and to activate specialist units, such as the Special

Operations Group (SOG), the police were also taking calls from terrified people, people in fear of their lives and who had seen horrific things.

The Tasmania Police Force had a total strength of just over 1000 men and women, and what was to become known as the Port Arthur massacre would involve almost 500 of them. They would also draw on specialist units from Victoria and New South Wales.

The isolation of the 500-square-kilometre peninsula, and the risks and challenges that posed in the event of a major crime or natural disasters such as bushfires, had long been recognised by Tasmania's emergency services, and the area had often been the focus of desktop and practical exercises. In the aftermath of the Hilton Hotel bombing in Sydney in 1975, Canberra and the States established the Standing Advisory Committee on Commonwealth/State Co-operation for Protection against Violence (SAC-PAV), and regular combined exercises were held throughout Australia under its auspices. The aim was to sharpen skills, co-operation and preparedness to cope with acts of terrorism or other major incidents.

Involvement in these national and local exercises was to prove invaluable as Tasmania Police set about managing the Port Arthur massacre. The responses were to work so well that there were times when it all seemed like an exercise, despite the enormity of all that had happened.

In the hours ahead, the then Deputy Commissioner Richard McCreadie called on Victoria for help in the first real test of cross-border co-operation. The Victorians sent their special operations group and two media liaison officers, and New South Wales flew in a team of expert crime examiners plus two media officers, while special equipment was supplied from Canberra. It proved to be an outstanding success.

At 1.57 p.m. there was a report that a car was on fire in the grounds of the Seascape guest house, 2.5 kilometres north of the historic site. It was but one of hundreds of phone calls pouring in to the police communications room in Hobart. To add to the confusion, there were reports from the Fox and Hounds Hotel, 800 metres from Seascape, that four wounded people had arrived on the doorstep after being shot at by a gunman standing on the highway as they drove past Seascape on their way to Port Arthur.

ABC television reporter Alison Smith had started her Sunday shift in the Hobart newsroom at 8.30 a.m. Like most Sundays, time had dragged. There were a couple of small media conferences, but otherwise it was quiet.

But at about 2.10 p.m., two ambulances raced past the building heading for the Tasman Bridge and Hobart's eastern shore. Smith decided there must have been a road accident, and two vehicles suggested it might be a bad one. She rang ambulance headquarters to check. There had been a shooting at Port Arthur, with as many as six people shot, she was told.

With a cameraman and a soundman, she was on her way. As they drove, Smith checked through a telephone directory, and on her mobile phone rang numbers in the Port Arthur area to try to get a lead on what had happened.

Out in the suburbs, Terry McCarthy, a sergeant in the police force and a police negotiator, was sprawled on a beanbag in his loungeroom watching the telecast of the AFL game between Brisbane and Fitzroy at the 'Gabba. He didn't usually bother watching football but his brother, John, was in the Fitzroy team that day, and Terry wanted to see how he went.

Terry McCarthy might have been out and about with his wife and three-year-old son that day. Perhaps they might have gone to Port Arthur. It was a popular destination for the family: their active youngster liked the space. But the little boy had stayed overnight with his grandmother and, by the time she returned him, it was too late to think of the 100 kilometre drive to Port Arthur.

Twenty-five minutes into the first quarter, McCarthy's phone rang: "Twenty dead at Port Arthur. Get here now."

The efforts of ABC reporter Alison Smith to get through to anyone at Port Arthur were unsuccessful. Either the numbers didn't answer, or they rang out. She decided to try other addresses on the Tasman Peninsula, and dialled the number of Seascape, Sally and David Martin's guest house 2.5 kilometres from the historic site.

It was between 2.20 and 2.30 p.m. Smith and the cameraman and soundman were near Copping. The number took some time to answer. When the phone was eventually picked up, the response on the other end was strange, then chilling.

Smith heard laughter as if she had interrupted somebody in the middle of a joke, and the laughing became louder. Then it stopped. "Hullo," a man's voice said.

"Is this Seascape guest house?" Smith inquired.

There was more laughter. "Yes," came the reply.

"Who is this speaking?" the journalist asked.

There was more laughter, then the voice responded, "You can call me Jamie."

Smith began to realise something was very, very wrong. It wasn't the way a guest house owner would respond to a caller. She identified herself as being from the ABC and asked him what was happening.

Again there was laughter from the other end of the phone. "What's happening is that I'm having lots of fun, but I really need to have a shower. And if you try to call me again, I'll shoot the hostage." Smith froze. The next few seconds seemed like an eternity as she clutched the phone, not daring to speak. All she could hear was his breathing. Then the line went dead.

The ABC crew stopped the car and phoned police headquarters, which was by then being flooded with desperate calls from in and around Port Arthur.

At 2.50 p.m., police officer Terry McCarthy reported to Assistant Commissioner Luppo Prins, who was running the major incident room. Prins told him that a gunman, and perhaps others, could be at a property called Seascape. Some of the information had come from a journalist who had phoned the guest house, Prins said.

There was some confusion. The police didn't really know how many gunmen there were, or how many crime scenes. There was also no way of immediately confirming that the gunman holed up in Seascape was the same one responsible for the shootings at Port Arthur.

Police were also concerned that the man at Seascape might escape before the Special Operations Group being rushed to the area by helicopter and road could seal off the property.

The death and injury toll was mounting by the minute, and the number of crime sites was also growing. If more than one gunman was loose, there might be a shoot-out taking place in and around Seascape.

CHAPTER 17

....

The Negotiator

Over the twenty-four hours that followed, half of Tasmania's entire police force of 1000 men and women became involved.

The immediate problems facing the police command in Hobart were time and distance, the struggle to determine just what had happened, the developing siege of Seascape and the necessity to isolate the gunman.

It was now apparent that the gunman, using high-powered military style weapons, had killed at least thirty-two people and had wounded possibly twenty more at Port Arthur and along the short stretch of the Arthur Highway between there and Seascape. The carnage had occurred in less than thirty minutes and was spread over four crime scenes. All on a Sunday afternoon in an Australian state where a fatal road accident was about as tragic as a weekend could get on the police incident sheets. It was a situation so unbelievable that senior police and other emergency service personnel had initially believed, when they responded to phone calls and radio messages, that it was a training exercise.

With the Seascape site beside the Arthur Highway forming an armed stronghold controlling the direct approach to Port Arthur, reinforcements had to detour from the Taranna roadblock, 7 kilometres north, along the road to Nubeena, and then approach Port Arthur and Seascape from the south.

Inspector Peter Wild, the duty inspector that day, had made a high-speed dash towards Port Arthur and by 2 p.m. had set up a command post at the Tasmanian Devil Park at Taranna, 7 kilometres from Seascape. The park was the best choice for a forward command post, for two reasons. First, it sat beside the only road access to the rest of the peninsula. Second, the tourism venture had important infrastructure in a notoriously isolated area, including phones and a fax.

Superintendent Barry Bennett, the forward commander at Taranna, had been off duty when he phoned the radio room on Sunday afternoon and was told that several people had been shot at Port Arthur. He thought it was one of the SAC-PAV exercises. Well, okay, he thought. Just tell me where the exercise is and I'll get there.

"No boss, this one is fair dinkum," said the radio room operator.

In an unmarked car, Bennett reported for a briefing from Luppo Prins, then headed for Taranna. His first task was to make sure that the containment of Seascape was complete. He realised that with a prolonged siege likely, the Special Operations Group would need expert assistance, so asked that a request be made for help to Victoria. Plenty of information was coming in, but none of it had been confirmed.

An advance party of three of the 27-member Special Operations Group were sent by helicopter. They arrived at the forward command post at Taranna at about 3.15 p.m. Others followed in the squad's two Toyota Landcruisers, arriving at 4.12 p.m. Hank Timmerman, the SOG commander for just ten days, now had a team of thirteen in place. The first of them moved forward to Seascape just before 4 p.m. By 5.12 p.m., they were all in place.

The gunman had chosen his stronghold well, if what he had planned was a stand-off or a bloody shoot-out with police. The house was in the middle of a 2–4 hectare paddock which was mostly cleared. The bay was on one side. There were two other buildings on the block, but the gunman had 360-degree vision, and any approach would have to be made over distance across open ground. In daylight, the SOG marksmen could get no closer than 150 metres, even in full camouflage gear.

Timmerman had another problem: two uniform police, Garry Whittle and Pat Allen, were trapped in a roadside ditch. There was no way they could be rescued until after dark.

Pat Allen had been in the traffic office in Hobart with another officer, Perry Caulfield, when he had heard the first reports. They had headed for the scene. As they approached Seascape, they saw a vehicle on fire. They stopped and spoke to an SOG member, who told them that there were wounded people at the Fox and Hounds Hotel up the road, and that police were needed there as soon as possible. The four victims had apparently been wounded by shots fired by a gunman standing beside the highway outside Seascape as they drove towards Port Arthur shortly before 2 p.m. As horrific as some of the wounds were, those four people could count themselves fortunate to have survived the rampage.

Having learned this information from the SOG member, police officers Pat Allen and Perry Caulfield had a choice. They could go the back way via Nubeena to avoid Seascape, or go straight through. Allen had seen policeman Garry Whittle, who had been fired on by gunman as he drove along the highway beside Seascape, hiding behind his car. Caulfield and Allen sped past in the traffic division station wagon and drove straight to the Fox and Hounds.

There was an ambulance there and some wounded. It was mayhem. One man said to Allen, "Just be careful, cock. This guy's mad."

Leaving Caulfield behind, Allen set off back to assist Whittle. He realised Whittle would be very vulnerable, as he would be sitting on the side of the car facing Seascape, so he did a U-turn and drove back along the highway. He was near the driveway into Seascape when the gunman opened fire. He had the choice to go to his colleague's assistance or to play safe. But Whittle was by himself, so Allen took the dangerous course and went to him.

Whittle was in the muddy, leech-infested ditch. Allen scrambled in beside him after first remembering to grab a walkie-talkie from the station wagon. There was a concrete culvert which offered some protection. They were about 180 metres from the guest house. The firing continued.

The leeches soon made their presence felt, but there wasn't a lot either could do. Armed only with their pistols, the officers expected the gunman would emerge and attack them. They hurriedly worked out their options. It didn't take long, because there was nowhere to go. They could have dived into one of the cars and tried to take off, but it would have been too open. They decided that, if the gunman came after them, they would run towards him, firing their pistols, in a bid to keep his head down and capture him. It would be their only chance of survival: there was nowhere to run to, nowhere to hide, particularly with the power and the range of the weapons they were facing. Otherwise, if they waited where they were, they'd be shot down like dogs in a ditch.

The two men tried to keep up their spirits. Whittle joked that he was starving and might radio for a pizza. "Do you think they'll deliver?" he asked Allen. Were the possums scuttling about in the tree above them about to add to their discomfort by urinating on them? Allen asked his mate dryly.

Back in Hobart, police negotiator Sergeant Terry McCarthy was directed to grab the phone in the commander's office and try to establish whether the information about Seascape was correct. The number was engaged, or off the hook, but McCarthy kept trying.

In between dialling Seascape, McCarthy called more negotiators and soon managed to activate a full team. A police negotiator since 1989, McCarthy was on call that weekend as a team leader. A complete team comprised the leader, a primary negotiator, a secondary team leader and an assistant. Usually, the practice was to get the negotiators immediately to the scene in their specially equipped truck. But as Port Arthur was almost 100 kilometres away, Prins and McCarthy agreed that it was important to get some dialogue going with the gunman as soon as possible.

The plan was to establish a relationship with the gunman via the phone from Hobart, then hand over to another team once the truck was in position. Telstra was asked to isolate Seascape's phone to secure the link. The fact that the phone was engaged suggested that friends or neighbours of the Martins may have been ringing to check on their welfare.

Finally, McCarthy got through at 3.20 p.m. and spoke to the man, who identified himself as Jamie, for about ten minutes. Jamie lost no time in listing his demands. He said he had three hostages, and he wanted a helicopter to land beside the guest house between 11 p.m. and midnight to fly him to Hobart airport, where an Ansett flight was to be standing by to take him to Adelaide.

His approach surprised McCarthy. Jamie was clearly very calm, and from very early on McCarthy felt as though the man was almost playing to a script.

The negotiator's usual approach was take some time explaining to the person on the line who he was and what he did, and also to spend a little time finding out about the other person. But Jamie got straight to the point.

McCarthy asked him what had happened at Port Arthur, but the man denied any knowledge of anything. Instead, he told McCarthy that he had pulled a BMW over near Fortescue Bay by pointing a rifle, and that the car had been occupied by a man and wife and a small child, two or three years old.

He said he had taken the man to Seascape and had the owners of the property as hostages as well. McCarthy tried to find out from him why he had done it, but whenever it got a little bit difficult for him, Jamie changed the subject or ended the conversation.

While the police negotiator talked to the man, the Special Operations Group attempted to seal off the area.

There was a puzzling moment when the man said he needed some time to get himself organised and to do things, including have a shower. He indicated that he wanted to get clean, that he had had a shower earlier but felt he had to have another one. McCarthy arranged to talk again at 5 p.m.

"How's things going in there, mate?" McCarthy asked on one occasion.

"Fine. Couldn't be better. Just like on a Hawaiian holiday," Jamie responded.

"Hawaiian holiday?" McCarthy queried, trying to keep the man talking in the hope of garnering more information.

"Yes, that's correct, sir."

"Oh, sorry. I don't understand what you mean by that," said McCarthy.

"Uh, I don't know myself," came the odd reply.

In between calls the gunman was occasionally firing shots from Seascape, but he was always careful to stand well back behind the curtains as he fired.

In one discussion, Jamie told McCarthy that he planned to take Sally Martin with him on the helicopter and to let the other two go.

Asked why she was to be the hostage, he replied: "Oh, she's easy, isn't she. She's a female, isn't she. I mean, she won't lash out at me."

The man also mentioned that not all the guns he had were his, because he had found some upstairs. David Martin and his sons, Glenn and Darren, had a collection of shotguns and rifles – some were family heirlooms. Jamie had also found a considerable amount of ammunition.

The man sounded quite young, and there were periods when he became almost petulant, childish. McCarthy's challenge was to keep him talking, to draw out information about his identity, his plans and the condition of the hostages.

Negotiating is a tough and stressful business, but McCarthy found attempting to defuse crisis situations challenging. His eight years in the traffic branch had been good preparation, as he often had to deal with drunks picked up by the breathalyser. Drunks, he knew, were by far the most difficult people to talk to, but he was a great believer that if you took time out to talk to somebody and explain things, you could calm them down.

Soon after nightfall, Jamie claimed that he was going to fry some bacon and eggs for the hostages. "It's all I can find that's nutritious," he said.

But McCarthy came to suspect that all three hostages were dead. Very early on in the negotiations McCarthy had formed the opinion that there was nobody else alive in the place. This was brought home to him when Jamie talked of "transporting" one of the hostages into a room. It was such an unusual word to use. The man had indicated that he had Sally Martin in the room with him, but when McCarthy asked to talk to her, he was told that she was half asleep and in no position to talk.

As McCarthy continued the talks, three of the negotiating team, using leads off the line, were listening intently for background sounds which would indicate the presence of another person. Phones are surprisingly good at detecting background noise, but there were no sobs, no crying – nothing.

Around 6.30 p.m., a call to Hobart headquarters from a member of the public in Hobart suggested that a man called Martin Bryant could be the person holed up in Seascape because he had an obsession about the owners, David and Sally Martin. It was but one of a number of tips provided by members of the public that night. Martin Bryant's passport had also been found in the Volvo abandoned beside the toll booth at the entrance to the historic site. However, it was not until about 8.30 p.m., when details of the vehicle's registration came through confirming Bryant as the owner, that police finally knew the identity of the person they were dealing with. It made little difference to the negotiating team: their aim always was never to divulge how much they knew about the individual they were dealing with.

Throughout the series of calls that afternoon and evening, the man maintained that he was in no way involved in anything that had happened at Port Arthur.

"I was hoping you might be able to tell me a little bit about what happened at Port Arthur," said McCarthy.

"Was there anyone hurt?" Jamie asked.

"Well, I understand there's been a number of people hurt."

"Yeah. Oh, they weren't killed?"

"Well, I don't know that. I don't know the full details. I know that somebody's been shooting people down at Port Arthur, and in the meantime we've also encountered the problem that we have you ... you sort of, er, want a helicopter and all these things, and we're trying to establish whether the incidents are connected in any way."

"No, no, they're not at all. I don't know who that person was, but what I can guarantee you is that I'm looking forward to my helicopter ride ... Hey, I've got to go 'cause this kettle's squealing downstairs. I'm making a cuppa tea for the hostages."

Later, McCarthy asked Bryant whether he had met Sally Martin before that day.

"Oh, I've known her all my life. Yeah. She's been bad news to me."

Pressed to explain, he began to ramble, saying Sally Martin had hurt him and his father. "You'll find out that they had a farm up Palmers Lookout Road – that lovely quaint old place. She's got two boys ... She's going to keep it anyway."

He claimed that his father had been going to buy the property but had missed out "because she started causing trouble ... she's a troublemaker. She's part Jewish, you know."

He said he detested Jews and had been snubbed by a Jewish couple in Miami while he waited to go on a cruise. "I met up with this couple and when this other chap walked along and started talking to them, well, they more or less dumped me."

Bryant suddenly broke off this discussion claiming he had heard noises. He became agitated and threatened that if police were creeping up on Seascape he would blow the hostages' brains out. McCarthy reassured him no such attempt was being made. Martin Bryant calmed down, saying it might have been rabbits or the wind that he had heard.

Throughout the exchanges, Bryant referred to Glenn Pears, the third hostage, as "Rick", but wouldn't discuss the "kidnap" at Fortescue Bay. Instead, he kept returning to the subject of the helicopter, saying he'd once paid $35 each for himself and his girlfriend to have a helicopter ride at Bushy Park in Tasmania's Derwent Valley.

"I've got so many books on helicopters you've got no idea ... I missed out on one about four years ago. I was going to buy one for $95,000. It was advertised in the *Mercury*. I missed out. I'm very upset about that."

He again became very agitated at the start of their next phone call, claiming he had spotted a police marksman. McCarthy guessed it was probably a small red light on a radio on the SOG marksman's back — a light which is normally taped over during operations.

"Ask him to move on ... he's gonna shoot, he's trying to shoot ... I'll blow this ... you know, you know what's gonna happen if ... "

McCarthy agreed to have the officer moved back. Bryant accepted the assurance, but warned that if it was not completed within ten minutes, the hostages would die. Moments later he stepped up the pressure: "If you don't call him off in five minutes, man, they're all dead."

"Okay, just take it easy, Jamie."

Martin Bryant laughed. "All right. I'll get back in touch with you in twenty-five minutes ... "

But during their next contact he introduced a frightening new element — the claim that he had found two boxes of gelignite and was prepared to blow himself up, "if it came to that". He said he had opened one box and seen a Chinese label.

Brushing aside McCarthy's concerns, Bryant continued to push for more information on the helicopter. After the call ended, he fired more shots, moving from room to room, but always taking care to stand well back from the windows.

During their last conversation, which ended soon after 9 p.m., he said he would be armed only with a 15-inch knife when he boarded the helicopter with Sally Martin. He would break up his guns before leaving.

"Okay," said McCarthy. "What are you going to do with them after you destroy them? Are you going to throw them outside so that we know they're all outside before you go to the aircraft?"

"I can do that. Yeah. Would you like me to do that?"

McCarthy agreed, and sought an assurance from Bryant that he wouldn't try anything. Police didn't want to see anybody hurt, particularly "Jamie", McCarthy said. "We certainly don't want to endanger anybody's life."

"I mean it's not only dying; it's the pain that people can inflict," said Bryant.

"I don't want anybody to suffer any pain. Do you?" McCarthy asked.

"No. I don't."

Soon afterwards, Martin Bryant ended the conversation, promising to call back at 10 p.m. But the negotiating team waited in vain. Apparently Bryant had been using a cordless phone, and it had lost battery power. It could have been recharged sufficiently if it had been placed back on its stand, but he was obviously unfamiliar with cordless phones. The negotiating team had assumed he was using a conventional handset.

Backed by other team members, plus a Hobart psychiatrist, Ian Sale, and the police psychologist Mike Ryan, McCarthy had had six separate conversations with the man.

During the night the negotiating team was fed information as it was gathered by other police. Some people had suggested that Bryant was a simpleton, that he was a bit slow on the uptake. But McCarthy wondered whether the man hadn't been misjudged over the years. He'd found that parts of his conversation seemed prepared in advance, and it had become clear that some of what Bryant had done was extremely well planned.

CHAPTER 18

Military Tactics

At around 10 p.m., two SOGs crawled 300 metres to extract the police officers Allen and Whittle from their ditch. The two trapped men had maintained contact via a walkie-talkie.

Allen and Whittle, guided by the SOGs, then crawled almost 200 metres to safety. It felt like 200 miles. But the eight or so hours in the ditch had passed quite quickly. It had been muddy, wet and cold, but to the two officers it hadn't seemed that long.

Superintendent Barry Bennett, who was in charge of the forward command post at Taranna, had been the previous SOG commander and had a keen understanding of the difficulties presented by the site and the possibility of an extended operation. At about 5 p.m., Timmerman had asked Bennett about the possibility of getting help from the Victoria Police SOG. He felt that given the site and the firepower the gunman had already demonstrated, eight to ten hours was about as long as his own men could operate at peak efficiency.

Two teams of ten men were immediately dispatched from Melbourne, and arrived at Seascape by 1 a.m. It was an extraordinarily fast response.

There had been a minor hiccup at Hobart. The Victorian officers had had to be sworn in so they could legally operate in Tasmania. Police Commissioner John Johnson was on hand to greet them, but it took a few minutes to find a Bible for the ceremony.

Once at Seascape, the Victorians were deployed one on one with a Tasmanian counterpart. The forces merged well, and Timmerman was pleased to have the experience and co-operation of his Victorian counterpart, Acting Chief Inspector Don Stokes. Some of the Tasmanians were withdrawn for some hot food and a short rest when the Victorians took up positions.

At times, Bryant was caught in the sights of some of the marksmen, but there was never a suggestion that he be shot. There are national guidelines for the use of force, and every State is a signatory to those guidelines. Officers cannot kill anyone unless their life is in immediate danger, or the lives of others are in immediate danger.

During those first few hours, and for much of the night, Bryant seemed to be toying with the Special Operations Group. He moved from room to room, flicking lights on and off and acting like somebody who had read a lot of war stories and picked up some military tactics.

But he never ever presented himself as a target at a window; instead he always stood a couple of metres back and fired from there. Only the flash of the muzzle blast could be seen as he fired a few rounds, put the gun down, crawled along to the next gun, and fired again: Bryant ensured he was never seen himself. It appeared his intention was to make police think there was more than one gunman in Seascape.

After dark, for a short time they believed there *were* more than one gunman, as firing came from beside the chimney of another building on the property. Then a marksman spotted Bryant running between it and the main house. He had another ploy, which was to switch on a light in a room on the bottom floor, then run upstairs and fire random shots. At one stage the electricity supply to the house was cut off on police instructions. But the move blacked out all of Port Arthur, and the supply was quickly restored to the already shocked and nervous community. In all, Bryant fired some 250 rounds from his own two guns and from the weapons he found stored in Seascape.

At 7.37 a.m. there was a series of shots fired from the house. Eight minutes later smoke was seen coming from an upstairs window. The Port Arthur and Eaglehawk Neck volunteer fire brigades were put on stand-by. Among their crews were personal friends of Seascape's owners, David and Sally Martin. As the flames took hold, police reported that someone seemed to be going berserk, with furniture and other objects being hurled from the windows. More shots were heard, and someone thought they could hear shouting.

The sight of smoke curling from part of Seascape put police in a very difficult position, particularly the new forward commander Bob Fielding and the SOG commander Hank Timmerman. Were the hostages still alive? If so, could they be retrieved from the burning building? And at what cost? Superintendent Fielding, who had taken over from Barry Bennett at 3.35 a.m., was the man who had to make the decision. He was told there were probably two hostages in the house and that there might also be a third, though that person (Glenn Pears) could be in the boot of the burnt-out BMW nearby.

An assault on Seascape would mean putting into action the SOG's emergency plan. The plan was simple: drive straight down the driveway as fast as possible with the officers clinging to the four-wheel drives and holding ballistic shields as protection. It would be virtually "crash bash" into the house, with fourteen police taking part. But they estimated that the results would be catastrophic. A third of the police would be casualties, almost certainly killed, given the power of the weapons Bryant was using. The only other alternative was to attempt to approach Seascape by stealth, crawling through the bush and along the creek, and hope to isolate the hostages from the gunman. But when the smoke was seen, the whole situation changed.

Back at the forward command post, Bob Fielding was in constant communication with the SOGs. He knew that Bryant was still firing shots as the flames spread. If the hostages were still alive, time was running out fast.

Down the line again came a call from the SOGs: "Will we go in, boss? Do you want us to go in?"

The troops were obviously as concerned as Fielding that there were people in the house who were possibly being burned alive.

A psychiatrist who had been helping police since the previous afternoon told Fielding that he thought it possible the hostages were still alive. "You've got to send the SOG in."

"Make your mind up! You told me ten minutes ago that you were satisfied they were dead. Well, are they or aren't they? What's your best estimate of it?" Fielding snapped back. It was a measure of the tension and pressure that had been building since the previous afternoon.

Fielding had to make the decision. But even as reports of the flames and more gunfire were relayed to his command post, he realised that he couldn't order the SOG to attack. A full-on assault on Seascape would have meant sending several police to their deaths. And there was also the chance that the entire building was booby-trapped. He rationalised it this way: he could justify his actions to the hostages' relatives far more easily than to the families of the police who would have been killed in the assault.

But the SOG men weren't shirking the issue. Everyone on the perimeter around Seascape was ready to do his job and follow an order to attack, even though they were dreading that command coming down the line.

Finally, Bryant emerged from Seascape at 8.24 a.m., his clothing alight. At first it was thought that he was armed with a handgun and firing it. The police lost sight of him in the smoke for several seconds, and when he reappeared he had torn off his clothing and was naked. In those first few moments, there was no way of being absolutely certain that it was the hostage-taker who had emerged. That raised the dilemma: should police be ordered forward to rescue the "hostage" and run the risk of coming under fire from the house?

As they watched, the man fell over and began writhing on the ground. There was no sign of a gun or a knife, but after all that had gone on, the police were cautious. To add to the threat and confusion, ammunition was exploding in the blazing house.

Satisfied that Bryant wasn't armed, the SOGs swooped in a three-vehicle dash down the driveway. A team of four men handcuffed him with plastic strips and bound his legs. It was 8.37 a.m. The siege of Seascape was over.

The house was now engulfed in flame, making it impossible for the other SOGs to get into the building to search for the hostages. Bryant lay quietly on the ground, though he was obviously in pain from serious burns to his back and buttocks. He was picked up and taken to an ambulance, where paramedics were waiting. They had slept in their ambulance overnight.

One of them, Peter Stride, had seen the man before. He had helped cut him out of a car after a road smash. It was the accident in which Helen Harvey had been killed near Copping in October 1992.

Later, the remains of David and Sally Martin and Glenn Pears were found in the ruins of the burnt-out guest house. All three had been shot, Pears with his hands handcuffed behind his back. David Martin may also have been stabbed, and Sally Martin had been struck with a blunt object.

CHAPTER 19

Innocence Lost

When Walter Mikac, Nanette Mikac's husband, and father of Alannah and Madeline, heard there had been some incident at Port Arthur, he immediately rang home. There was no answer. Warning bells rang. With his father-in-law, he set off for Port Arthur.

In the car park they found Nanette's car, and their fears grew. Walter began to search frantically for his family. He met some friends, Stephen and Pam Ireland, the peninsula's husband and wife medical team. They'd been called to Port Arthur at about 3 p.m. and had driven straight to the Broad Arrow Café. On the way down the road from the toll booth they had noticed one group of four bodies, then another group of three. At the Broad Arrow they had joined two retired surgeons, ambulance officers and first aid workers, and had begun to attend to those who were most seriously injured.

Early that Sunday evening, when all the wounded had been transferred to Hobart by helicopter, ambulances and bus, Pam Ireland found Walter Mikac still searching for his family. She had an eerie and sad feeling that the three bodies they had driven past on the way to attend the wounded could be the Mikacs.

With Stephen and some ambulance officers and police she walked back up the road and found Nanette and the children. Pam then had to return to Walter to tell him of his terrible loss.

On Monday morning, as police and forensic experts prepared to complete their examinations of the Port Arthur site, Walter Mikac came to grieve beside the bodies of his wife and children. It was a moment that the already stressed investigators would never forget.

Superintendent Bob Fielding, the police forward commander, also visited the Port Arthur site on that Monday morning to inspect the scene and to offer support to those on duty, some of whom had guarded the bodies throughout the night.

Nightfall had meant that the full crime-scene investigation could not be completed until daylight, so none of the bodies could be moved. Fielding realised what a horrendous experience that must have been, not only for young police, but also for the veterans.

The Superintendent later bumped into one of the officers who had been there that night guarding the bodies. He was an old hand, a policeman with years of experience. Fielding asked him how he was feeling. "Look, boss, I didn't like to say to you yesterday that I was finding it particularly hard."

Fielding said that was okay, he wouldn't have expected him to find it easy.

"You know what really got to me? I'm not sure which of the Mikac girls it was, but it was one of them. I went up and I had to lift the little hand to put the tag on and she was wearing the same clothes and shoes as my little granddaughter. I just went blank. I thought it was my granddaughter lying there."

PART III
A Nation in Shock

PART III

1961

A Nation in Shock

CHAPTER 20

At the Royal Hobart Hospital

Martin Bryant was admitted to the Royal Hobart Hospital burns unit late on Monday morning. He was handcuffed to the bed and put under strict guard. The following day he was charged with the murder of Kate Scott, twenty-one, of Western Australia.

On the hospital's third floor, the burns unit offered both the facilities to treat his injuries and the isolation and security required. Police, security men and prison officers kept the area sealed off to all except medical staff.

A decision was made that only senior staff would be called upon to treat Bryant and that any of them would be free to refuse. Some did. The hospital was not prepared to force people to compromise their own personal feelings.

The treatment of Martin Bryant involved none of the rapport that is usually established with a seriously ill patient. Instead, it was skilled but detached.

Bryant's presence worried some of the wounded, and upset relatives of the dead and injured. Like the rest of Australia, staff and patients were rarely far from a television set or radio in the first days after the shootings. The news was always the same. Always the flashback to 1.30 p.m., Sunday, 28 April.

Hobart has no separate morgue. So late on Monday evening the first twenty bodies had been brought to the hospital's mortuary. Staff faced the task of preparing and processing the paperwork and taking descriptions of each of the bodies.

The hospital's forensic pathologist, Tim Lyons, had been at the scene since Sunday afternoon. None of the bodies could be moved until the crime scene investigation had been completed.

By Tuesday, grieving relatives were flocking to the Royal from all parts of Australia, as well as from overseas. To help lessen the suffering of the families, each body was moved upstairs, away from the mortuary, to viewing beds surrounded by flowers in individual rooms. Grieving relatives and friends could stay as long as they wanted. Nurses volunteered to assist them and were briefed by the hospital's social workers and pastoral care people. The hospital also provided specialist counsellors.

For the first time in its long history, the hospital was the target of a mounting tide of community anger. Distraught at the loss or injury of friends or family, some people wanted to know why the gunman was being cared for, particularly in the same place, on the same floor, as some of his victims. One wall of the hospital was daubed with the grim message "An Eye for an Eye". As the threats and bomb hoaxes began, security was strengthened.

It was an almost intolerable situation for doctors, nurses, administration staff, cleaners and kitchen hands. One hospital worker reported that her child was taunted at school.

The Royal had known nothing like this before. The kind of responses it had inspired in the public in the past were letters and messages of thanks in the classified columns of the local newspaper, the *Mercury*, for kind and caring treatment. Tasmanians were proud of their major hospital. "If you're crook, it's the only place to be," newcomers were often told.

Some of the medical staff found grim humour in the continuing threats. One joked that it looked like Code Brown was to be put through its paces again, if any of the bomb hoaxes proved to be real.

But by the middle of that first week the pressures were beginning to hit hard. Staff who had opened the week with seventeen or eighteen hours straight were starting to drop. Now the world's media were at the front door, and the lawns were sporting satellite dishes. Television crews and newspaper and magazine photographers had the place staked out. The hospital's chief executive, Lindsay Pyne, became the Royal's talking head, and the senior doctors gave regular reports to media conferences.

Pyne felt the full brunt of the bomb threats because it was his responsibility to decide what action should be taken. Evacuate or not? The Royal is a 500-bed hospital and none of the threats was specific as to what area was allegedly targeted. He had to make a judgment about each threat, realising that if he ignored one, and it turned out to be real, the result would be unbearable. By the fourth bomb threat he wondered whether he was making informed decisions.

The transfer of Bryant to Risdon gaol the following Sunday eased some of the pressures, and ended the need for stringent security. It felt as if a dark cloud had been lifted.

The sense of co-operation among the hospital's 1900 staff helped them cope with the pressures surrounding the Port Arthur tragedy. But what kept them all going was the amazing response from Australia and the rest of the world. So many flowers were sent that a plea was finally issued requesting that well-wishers make a gift to the Port Arthur appeal instead. The staff and owners of Mure's Seafood Restaurant on Hobart's dockside sent a trolley of seafood to the team manning the ward in which the Port Arthur wounded lay. Every patient received a tropical flower flown down from north Queensland. There were letters, cards and gifts. So much chocolate arrived from a donor interstate that it had to be distributed throughout the hospital.

And then there were letters from the children all over the country who had heard on television or read in the newspapers that the Royal Albert Hospital had received threats for treating Bryant.

> Dear Hospital Staff,
> Thank you for trying to save injured people in the Port Arthur massacre. Some people in our grade were told that you were getting complaints about treating Martin Bryant, and I feel sorry for you.
> Yours sincerely,
> Ebony Watson, Altona Primary School.

Ebony's letter was accompanied by a drawing showing a nurse, an ambulance and a smiling sun.

Luke Watson, from the same school, sent with his letter a drawing of trees, sunshine and a plane.

> Dear hospital staff,
> Thank you for saving the injured people. I was very sad when I saw the Port Arthur massacre on the news.

These were two of forty letters and drawings received from the Victorian school of Altona Primary, and to the health workers at the Royal it meant a lot. The hospital wrote back to every child, and included a Tasmanian badge with each letter. The messages from the children, and the letters and faxes from all around the world, provided a great boost to morale.

Some of them came from the picturesque market town of Dunblane, in Scotland, where on 13 March 1996 a teacher and sixteen five-year-old children had been shot dead and twelve of their classmates wounded in the school gymnasium. The gunman, a 43-year-old bachelor named Thomas Hamilton, had then shot himself.

Another important contribution came from the Western General Hospital in Melbourne and the Launceston General Hospital. Several nurses from Launceston drove south, and doctors and nurses from the Western flew to Hobart to donate their time and to work half-shifts so their Hobart counterparts could have a break. The major airlines flew them free, and Hobart's Hotel Grand Chancellor provided free accommodation. That support, those few hours break, the opportunity to get away and unwind, or at least try to understand what they had gone through, was invaluable.

Two days after the shootings, a letter signed by thirty-one members of the Royal's medical staff was published in the Hobart newspaper, the *Mercury*:

Amid the carnage of the devastating slaughter at Port Arthur, we, as medical staff of the Royal Hobart Hospital, demand that Tasmania's politicians act now to ban civilian possession of automatic and semi-automatic weapons.

Assault rifles are made for one purpose only; to kill people. They have no other function. We have nothing but disgust for the failure of Tasmania's politicians to act before now. They have contributed to untold loss and grief.

CHAPTER 21

A Sorrow Never Known

The events of 28 April left a nation in shock, and nowhere was the sense of horror, disbelief and fear stronger than on the Tasman Peninsula itself. The people of the peninsula had lost family and friends, along with the security they had all grown up with. It was a loss of innocence; a deep and numbing shock. What only days before had seemed like an impossibility, like something that only happened somewhere else, had somehow happened to them. In a single afternoon the peace was shattered by a crime that would go down as the worst civilian shooting by a lone gunman in world history. Thirty-five dead, twenty-one wounded.

On the Wednesday following the massacre a state service was held at St David's Cathedral in Hobart. The centre of the city was silent as the service began, with families and friends of the victims occupying many of the pews, among them Mick Sargent and his friends John Riviere and Caroline

Villiers. The depth of the community's grief and the shock being felt by all Tasmanians was palpable.

Tiered seating was erected in Murray Street outside the cathedral, and the service was relayed to the several thousand people who gathered there.

The evening before, Dr Stuart Blackler, the Dean of Hobart, had walked out into Murray Street and watched workmen assembling the seating and erecting barricades. It was a perfect autumn night, clear and crisp, but despite the activity the street was almost quiet. There was none of the usual workplace banter. It was as if Murray Street had been turned into a sacred place by the community.

At the service, the Governor General, Sir William Deane, and the Prime Minister, John Howard, joined friends and relatives of the bereaved, emergency service workers, and other Tasmanians. The Anglican Bishop of Tasmania, the Right Reverend Phillip Newell, said: "The destruction of beautiful lives and the wastefulness of it all have immersed us in a sorrow we have never known before."

Outside the cathedral, the Prime Minister stopped to talk to some of the emergency service people and doctors who had been involved in Port Arthur. The image of Mr Howard comforting a doctor appeared around the world and helped symbolise the extent of community grief.

The doctor, Brian Walpole, a staff specialist at the Royal Hobart Hospital, later recalled that Mr Howard had walked past, then looked at him. "He gave me a sort of a quizzical look, and said some comforting words ... something like 'Hang on old boy, it'll all come good.' I saw the lump in his throat, and for a moment I sort of disintegrated. I suppose it was the look of empathy on his face."

Tasmania had rarely rated a news mention on the other side of Bass Strait. And now, suddenly, it was the focus of the world's media: the BBC had broadcast the news within forty-five minutes, and in the United States the story was a major item on television for three consecutive days.

It was against this background that the community recovery program had begun within ninety minutes of the killings. Within the various emergency services, critical incident stress debriefing teams began debriefing police, ambulance personnel and volunteer firemen. Eight community counsellors had been sent from Hobart to the Tasman Peninsula that fateful afternoon.

A major counselling debrief had been arranged that night at the Police Academy at Rokeby, on Hobart's outskirts, for relatives of the victims and witnesses to the tragedy. Twenty trauma counsellors took part and assisted 120 people. In addition, another twelve counsellors manned a police hotline on that Sunday night to speak to relatives and friends of victims, ringing from all over Australia and overseas. Calls to that 24-hour hotline averaged forty-eight minutes each.

Counselling teams were sent to two major Hobart hotels to assist tourists, and arrangements were made for transport and accommodation for many of the interstate visitors who had witnessed the horror at Port Arthur. Altogether, there were 463 members of staff from state and Commonwealth departments, non-government organisations and private practitioners involved in the recovery strategies from 28 April to 10 May. The vast majority of these had expertise in psychology, psychiatry, trauma or critical incident stress counselling.

Three counselling teams travelled from Hobart to Nubeena each day, and counsellors and administrative staff were debriefed at the end of each shift. A key part of the community recovery arrangements were two briefings to television, radio and print journalists and other personnel on the importance of their role in aiding community and personal recovery.

A network was established for trauma counselling information and advice for people throughout Australia affected by the events of 28 April. Victims and others affected also received a regular newsletter to keep them up-to-date with issues such as the Port Arthur appeal, legal issues surrounding the case, criminal injuries compensation and ongoing counselling.

In Tasmania, a series of pamphlets were produced covering such matters as "the family and personal crisis", "children and trauma", and "coping with a tragic event".

The emergency services, and the community in general, also benefited from the messages of sympathy and support which flooded in from all over the world. The Premier, Tony Rundle, received hundreds of letters and cards expressing sympathy to Tasmania and friends and relatives of the victims. Bill and Margaret Moore wrote from Dunblane, Scotland, in a letter dated 29 April:

> We are still coming to terms with the tragedy in our own community and we are still being sustained by the thoughts and prayers from all over the world. Our thoughts and prayers go to you, all Tasmanians, and particularly to the bereaved and survivors of your own tragedy.

The Premier of Bermuda, David Saul, said that the people of Bermuda were shocked and saddened by the tragic events.

> Justice will take its course in the fullness of time, but in the meantime our hearts go out to all those who were injured in the attacks, and our deepest sympathy is extended to the families of those who lost their lives.

Among the letters, cards and drawings from schoolchildren throughout Australia was one from 12-year-old Adam Fritsche, of North Curl Curl, New South Wales:

> I go to North Curl Curl Public School. We are all very, very sorry about this tragic event. I'm sorry for the people that died and were injured at Port Arthur. I wish I could do something more.

CHAPTER 22

Daffodils Will Bloom

"It's like in an afternoon my whole life's just been erased," Walter Mikac had told a national television audience on the night following the tragedy.

On 9 May, Nanette, Alannah and Madeline Mikac's funeral was held in Melbourne. Pastor Allan Anderson appealed to politicians: "Do not trade your votes for lives. Hold to your resolve to deal with this menace of unnecessary firearms in our society. Listen not to the loud calls of the few who want to selfishly keep their weapons, but instead hear the cries of those who have died, listen to the quiet sobs of those who live, see the majority who stand with them."

A few days before, the newly elected Prime Minister, John Howard, had announced plans for a meeting of state and federal police ministers to discuss a ban on automatic and semi-automatic weapons and a buy-back scheme funded by the federal government. Meeting the day after the Mikac funeral, the ministers agreed to the bans and the provision of a compensation scheme which would cost millions of dollars. The agreement drew a hostile reception from the gun lobby, but Tasmania acted immediately to toughen its previously lax laws on guns.

In July, Walter Mikac joined with the National Coalition for Gun Control at a number of public rallies. In Hobart on 18 July, supported by his brother, Steve, he held his first media conference and praised Prime Minister John Howard for his leadership. He called on other MPs to show some "intestinal fortitude". Then, on 23 July, Walter Mikac laid flowers on the steps of Parliament House in Hobart to remind the Legislative Council, which was then debating gun control, of the victims of the Port Arthur massacre.

Mikac took his message to rallies in Melbourne and Sydney on 28 July. In Sydney, 3000 people gathered at the Domain and heard him urge Australians to keep up the pressure for the promised gun control. "As you all know, three months ago to this day I lost the entire reason for my existence," he said.

At Port Arthur, three weeks after the shooting, 6000 people gathered for an ecumenical service in the grounds. They laid flowers around a simple wooden cross bearing the names of the thirty-five victims, and watched as thirty-five white pigeons were freed to circle the site. The day was an act of reclamation of Port Arthur by its staff and by visitors.

The Premier, Tony Rundle, told the crowd that there was no sense or reason for the wickedness that had occurred three weeks before. "Yet even on that blackest day there were great shafts of light. Wickedness passes, but courage, strength in adversity and hope for the future are with us forever.

In just twelve weeks the daffodils will bloom, and blossom will burst forth from the trees."

Neil Noye, the Tasman Peninsula's mayor, said that the small community had been dealt a fearful blow on 28 April and had wondered if life could ever be blacker. "We had never thought our beautiful peninsula would be the scene for such a horrific crime against humanity.

"Our confidence in the old solid values of life, held by people of goodwill everywhere, was badly shaken. How could we ever recover, we asked ourselves. While I never doubted recovery was possible, I looked to the hurdles we faced with some alarm.

"But today, less than a month on, we gather here as a community bound together by a common belief in the collective goodness of humanity. It's a belief that's been restored by the overwhelming goodwill shown to our community by fellow Australians and countless people overseas. In common Australian terms, our mates have not let us down. They have come forward with a deeply moving generosity of spirit to help us along the tough road to recovery. We could have asked for no more."

Mick Sargent, the keen drag racer from Perth who had lost his beloved Kate, had escaped with only minor physical injuries. In the days following the massacre, Mick's counsellor had initially become concerned about his refusal to return home to Perth. But Mick had no intention of leaving without Kate, and was awaiting the release of her body. He spent part of the time retracing everywhere they had been together in Hobart, including restaurants and Wrest Point. It seemed to be helping him in some way come to terms with what had happened, so the counsellor recommended that he continue.

He also re-visited the Port Arthur Historic Site. It really helped, but as he was sitting with a Salvation Army man near the information centre adjacent to the Broad Arrow, having a cup of coffee, he heard a loud bang behind him. Mick threw himself on the ground, but the sound was caused only by a small bough or a nut dropping onto a tin roof.

Back in Western Australia his family had become increasingly anxious and asked him to come back home. Kate's parents rang him and begged him to come home, assuring him that Kate would get home by herself. But he couldn't leave without her. They had gone to Port Arthur together, and they were coming home together. That was it.

Eight days after the tragedy, Mick Sargent took Kate Scott home.

At Royal Hobart Hospital, staff were deeply affected when they heard of the horror witnessed by their shocked and traumatised patients. As the names of the dead and wounded became known, more and more people had become caught up in the grief. It seemed that virtually everyone knew a victim, or a member of their family. One of the hospital's registrars was good friends with Glenn Pears and Zoe Hall.

Maree Broome, of Kilmore, Victoria, whose husband, Gary, was wounded, spent from eight o'clock in the morning to late at night in the ward with him each day, and would never forget the kindness and high standard of care. When a memorial service was conducted on the lawns below, she and her husband stood on a balcony of the hospital to watch.

One of the nurses looked up, and then the next minute she appeared beside them and put her arms around them.

There was also laughter to brighten the long days and nights in Ward 3A. Neville Quin had been stalked by the gunman and shot in the neck at close range by Bryant, who had said to him the moment before pulling the trigger, "No-one gets away from me." Despite his injury, Quin managed to reach his dying wife, Janet, who had been shot earlier. She died fifteen minutes later. He had learnt afterwards that, back home at Bicheno, his mother had collapsed and died when she heard of the shootings.

Despite his tragic personal loss and his own severe injuries, Quin kept the ward entertained, including his room-mate Gary Broome. Only four days after the shootings, he had joked about Gary to Gary's wife, Maree: "Oh, you've got a bit of a wacker there. I don't know how you stay married to him."

"Why? What's wrong," she had asked.

"We woke up at three this morning and couldn't sleep, so the girls made us a cup of tea. I looked over at Gary and there he was pouring his piddle bottle into his glass."

For the Reverend Glenn Cumbers, of the Church of Christ at Nubeena, the days immediately after the shootings passed almost in a blur as he counselled and comforted families, and organised funerals and a memorial service. Some days he made do with less than five hours' sleep, and struggled to come to terms with what he had experienced on 28 April. The images recurred again and again, and it would be months before he was able to sleep properly.

At the Port Arthur Historic Site itself, individual counselling and group therapy sessions were instigated to help staff cope with their grief. Ian Kingston, back on duty after the re-opening, had to re-live the events in a series of interviews as media focused on the first of the anniversaries, one hundred days after 28 April. Brigid Cook, hospitalised for a month after being shot in the thigh, returned to take charge of a tea rooms in the grounds. Some of Ian and Brigid's colleagues were unable to return to work; others were on special programs involving reduced hours or redeployment in other areas. The effects of post-traumatic stress disorder and clinical depression were being felt throughout the community, and the recovery process could not be measured in days or weeks or months.

A small group of staffers, including Brigid Cook and Wendy Scurr, were in the Supreme Court in Hobart on 30 September to hear Martin Bryant plead not guilty to seventy-two charges, including thirty-five of murder.

During the days that followed the disaster, those who had known Martin Bryant in the past struggled to make sense of the killings, and to come to terms with the fact that this young man had committed such senseless murder.

Bryant's girlfriend, Petra, was at home in the Huon when she had seen a television report about the Port Arthur shootings. When she heard that the gunman had mentioned something about wasps and Japs she knew it must have been Martin – it was something he often said.

Carleen Bryant had been desperately worried when she heard the news. Unable to contact her son by phone at his home, she had phoned Petra's family and asked if Petra would like to spend the night at her place. Petra's father had driven her to Carleen Bryant's home in Hobart's northern suburbs. Carleen had sought to reassure Petra and herself, saying it was possible Martin might have made a sudden decision to fly interstate; it was something he had done before. But their last hope had been dashed when police arrived at the house that terrible night.

In the first days and weeks after the shootings, both Petra and Carleen Bryant had been pursued by media but had declined to comment. Mrs Bryant had gone interstate for a few weeks after issuing a message of condolence to the victims, via her solicitor. She visited Martin a number of times in Risdon gaol. In a letter declining to be interviewed for this book, she attached a printed "Thank You" note dated June 1996. It said: "Words cannot express the sentiments and sympathy I have for the family, relatives and friends of the victims of Port Arthur." The note ended with Psalm 34, verses 17 and 18:

> The righteous cry out, and the Lord hears them,
> He delivers them from all their troubles,
> The Lord is close to the broken hearted,
> And saves those who are crushed in spirit.

Anitra and Harry Kuiper, the neighbouring family who had befriended Martin in New Town, wondered whether there was anything they or society in general could have done to prevent the massacre. And were they ever in danger? Perhaps they had been on Martin's list. Had he called by their home that day, only to find that they had left early for church?

The Kuiper children were sure that Martin would never have harmed them. For them, there were two Martin

Bryants: the Martin who played with them and bought them gifts, and the Martin who committed that horrendous crime.

In the months leading up to the murders, the Kuiper family had been shocked by the change in Martin Bryant. The young man who had always been so careful about his appearance and conscious of good clothes had begun to look scruffy. He had let his hair grow longer and he no longer dressed smartly. They had seen him once while shopping in the city and almost hadn't recognised him.

Harry Kuiper recalled another change. Instead of following his usual pattern and travelling everywhere by car, Bryant, for some reason known only to himself, had begun to catch buses, and there were stories that he was annoying female passengers and had been put off by the drivers a couple of times.

Five weeks before the shootings, Anitra Kuiper had gone shopping at Northgate shopping centre in Hobart's northern suburbs when someone came up behind her and put his arms around her. She didn't recognise the voice, and when she turned around and saw that it was Martin, she got quite a fright. It was as if he had wanted to shock her and was pleased that he had.

The Kuipers were convinced that Bryant was heavily influenced by violent videos. The Martin they knew was not capable of planning something like Port Arthur. They felt that he must have taken ideas from various videos – that he had watched them over and over and thought, "Yes, that looks good", and "Yes, that bit would be real cool."

They believed that Martin was in the United Kingdom around the time of the Dunblane massacre and would have been fascinated by all the attention the crime and the killer received. He would have thought it great to be the hero, the one everybody was talking about and writing about.

No, there was no way that society could have prevented the killings, they decided. The only way would be to lock up everybody who was slightly different, and it just wasn't possible. There were plenty of people out there like Martin, they felt, who would never hurt a fly.

For Glenn and Darren Martin, there was only one question: why?

They both remembered Martin Bryant on holidays at Port Arthur, a kid who was unable to mix in with a group.

There had been reports that Sally and David Martin had employed Martin Bryant to do odd jobs around the property, then had had a dispute with him and sacked him. Another story was that the Martins had cheated Bryant's father, Maurice, out of an opportunity to buy Seascape. It was said David and Maurice had been wharfies together and were friends and had a deal to go into partnership in Seascape.

Both Glenn and Darren had absolutely rejected claims that Bryant might have had a reason to kill their parents. Glenn and Darren were certain that Martin Bryant had never worked for their parents, either at Seascape or at the farm. Indeed, he had never set foot on the Seascape property. Neither was their father any more than an acquaintance of Maurice Bryant. David Martin had worked on the apple boats in Hobart as a shipwright while Maurice was a wharfie, but they had never mixed socially. Anyway, the Martins never went into partnerships with people. That wasn't their way.

Glenn was the first person to inform his parents that the old house was up for sale. At the Port Arthur store he used to cash cheques for an old wharfie who owned the property. The old man had told him he was planning to move back to town, and David Martin had known him from the wharf days. They hit it off well and the contract for sale was signed.

Perhaps the Martins were killed because Martin Bryant had a fixation on their farm near Port Arthur. When he was only about fifteen he would visit Glenn's shop to pick up newspapers and milk, and would ask Glenn to sell the farm to him. Of course Glenn didn't take his requests seriously, and assumed that his father might have put him up to it.

Bryant had occasionally played at the farm with Darren and other local youngsters when he was aged twelve or thirteen, but he was never permitted into the house itself. Sally Martin didn't trust the boy. Darren remembered her warning him to keep an eye on Martin whenever he was around. Sally Martin was recognised as a very good judge of character.

Then, in the mid-1980s, Sally told Darren during one of his weekend visits to the farm that Martin Bryant had been there and said he wanted to buy it. "Oh, get in line, Martin," she had joked in response. But for Martin Bryant perhaps it was just one more rejection, one more reason to hate Port Arthur.

Glenn Martin had last seen Bryant four or five months before 28 April, when Bryant had called at his coffee shop at Eastlands and ordered a sandwich and a roll. "How's Glenn these days?", Bryant inquired, and Glenn replied: "Oh, good. How are you? What are you doing these days?"

"I'm surfing and living off shares," Bryant answered, and that was the end of the conversation. Bryant and the girl he was with then sat quietly at a table eating the sandwich and roll. Then they left. Only after the Port Arthur shooting would Glenn Martin discover that his daughter, who runs a shop of her own in Sandy Bay, had also encountered Bryant some months before. Bryant had first asked her if she recognised him, then mentioned that he knew her father. He had begun to act strangely, and had upset the daughter and a customer with some of his comments. She became so concerned that she had phoned police. In retrospect it was another clue that Martin Bryant had been drifting out of control.

In the months following the fire, Glenn Martin spent some of his weekends sifting through the ashes looking for mementoes of his parents. The search yielded a pair of sewing scissors with Sally Martin's name on them, and a couple of small ornaments. One had survived the blaze in perfect condition – a small china piece which had been in the family's possession for many years. It was a miniature of the three wise monkeys: Hear no evil, see no evil, think no evil.

Glenn decided he would try to rebuild Seascape, even just as a shell, to cover the black scar left by the fire of 28 April.

It would be good for family members and for all the people of the Tasman Peninsula as they strove to recover from the horror of Martin Bryant's rampage. And that, he was sure, would be the way his parents would want it to be. He could hear them: "Don't look back; look forward. Get on with the job."

In a letter to the *Australian*, a Canadian woman who, with her husband, had spent Christmas Day and Boxing Day 1994 at Seascape, wrote:

Imagine two incredibly spry, grey-haired, inquisitive, talkative, trusting, grandparently hosts, who helpfully guided our stay in the area. Their kindness was immense; they prepared us for visiting the area by showing us a video with tea and biscuits. They recommended what to do and when; they arranged dinner reservations when most restaurants were closing down, and, finally, their breakfast repast was generous and the conversation so enjoyable that we nearly missed the morning tour of Port Arthur.

As I look at the picture of me and Sally standing on the front verandah of the quaint sea-shell pink cottage, I feel that the awful circumstances of their deaths should not go without a personal remembrance. May their families know that, half a world away, others cherish their memory and wish them eternal peace.

Maurice and Jillian Williams were two old acquaintances of Bryant's who had escaped his wrath that day. When they had returned home that fateful Sunday from a fortnight's holiday, they found knife marks in the door, as if someone had attempted entry. A burglar some time in the past fortnight, or a caller on 28 April?

They had reached the Taranna roadblock and heard what had happened that afternoon. They were told later that Bryant had been seen near their home that Sunday, which had left Jillian Williams wondering about two incidents a few weeks before the murders. One evening she and her married daughter had been followed along the beach by someone who then ran off when a car had approached. Then her young grand-daughter had been frightened by a face at the bedroom window. Mrs Williams said the child described the "bad man". When Bryant's picture was later published in the Hobart *Mercury*, the little girl had pointed to it and said, "That's the man that was looking in nanny's window."

The Williams had lived at the house for more than thirty years. They had first seen Bryant when he was eight or nine years old. Like others, they remembered the child who was always on the outer, seemingly unable to mix. The boy who was never still, who could never fit in with the other kids who played in the bush and on the beach every holiday and weekend, was unfailingly polite to adults. Indeed, you couldn't meet a more polite child.

But there was something odd about young Martin. It was those eyes, that look. He looked not at, but through a person, with those piercing blue eyes. There was something else: he hated tourists and was known to take his air gun to the main road and fire at their cars. He had owned an Osprey air rifle since he was ten years old, and sometimes he had fired it at the feet of other children to make them dance. Martin would also fire at tourists' cars as they drove past. Another favourite target was cats, and sometimes horses on a nearby farm. At the Port Arthur site itself he would sometimes spit at visitors. He hated Port Arthur, he hated the Broad Arrow and he hated tourists, Jill Williams remembered.

The reports that Bryant had commented about "Jap tourists" on 28 April had not surprised her. She remembered that Bryant's father, Maurice, had hated the Japanese, although no-one ever knew why.

Bryant was one of the few local youngsters not to earn pocket money by working at the Broad Arrow during the busy holiday seasons. But, as Janette Clark, a former Carnarvon Bay resident, remembered, Martin Bryant never needed the pocket money because whatever he wanted his parents would buy, no matter what the expense.

Mrs Williams, like the Larners, was sure that Martin Bryant had been looking for her and her husband on 28 April. For what reason? She recalled that when Bryant was a teenager, Maurice Williams had threatened to give him a boot up the bum if he ever again untied the Williams's boat from their private jetty. The boat had been left to float free a number of times.

After that reprimand, Bryant's mother came down to the Williams's house with Martin to tell Maurice Williams to stop picking on the boy. Mrs Williams remembered Martin Bryant standing behind his mother and grinning with that silly grin he had.

And there had been something else. Carleen Bryant's horse had bolted near tourists at the Port Arthur Historic Site, and the Parks and Wildlife rangers – of whom Maurice Williams was one – told her she would not be allowed to ride across the park again because of the risk to tourists. Trivial enough, but in the strange world of Martin Bryant it may have been just that – enough.

CHAPTER 23

The Port Arthur Taskforce

Now began the enormous task of investigating the shooting of each of the thirty-five people killed, and of those who were wounded.

All available evidence had to be collected, charges laid, and the prosecution case prepared. There had been six crime scenes over a distance of more than 2 kilometres, and hundreds of people – many from other states and some from other countries – had been caught up in the events.

On Thursday 2 May, four days after the massacre, Superintendent Jack Johnston, superintendent of operations support, had been told he had been selected to head a special task force to handle the case, and was given the go-ahead to select his team. Over the following fifteen weeks the taskforce collect more than 840 statements, travelling to every state and territory except the Northern Territory. Through Interpol, they also conducted inquiries in Sweden,

South Africa, the United States, Singapore, New Zealand and Malaysia.

Johnston, a 28-year veteran of the force, was an ideal choice to lead the taskforce and assemble its team members. He had excellent management skills and a reputation among the troops as a good boss – a bloke who got in and did the job, and expected everyone else to do the same.

Perhaps just as importantly, given the magnitude of the job, Johnston had a reputation for being somewhat of a futuristic thinker, someone with a keen appreciation of the value of computer technology in police work and some interesting ideas on how it might be extended. Johnston's sense of humour also took pressure off tense situations.

Johnston's decision virtually to manage the entire case with an innovative computer program designed by the team was a first for Australia and soon attracted strong interest from at least two states and the National Institute of Forensic Science in Canberra. The FBI also sought details.

The approach was unique in that it was the operational police, from himself down, who decided what the computer program would be. Rather than information technology experts outlining what they could have, team members determined what they wanted the system to do. The program was developed by Sergeant Robert Bonde, Constable Matthew Osborn, Sergeant Terry McCarthy, Constable Neville Matthew, and John Box and David Bowerman of the police information technology department.

Johnston's first move on that first Thursday was to call on three inspectors, John Maxwell, Ross Paine and John Warren; Maxwell to handle the administration and logistics, and Paine and Warren to look after the investigations. The following day the four sat down to hand-pick the rest of the team – nineteen police and three support staff. There was no argument as they ran through the names from the various police districts, and by mid-afternoon the phone calls were going out: "Report for duty with the Port Arthur Taskforce at headquarters on Monday morning."

From the outset there was a realisation that care had to be taken if stress was not to be a problem. Johnston was mindful that he and his colleagues didn't exert too much pressure on team members. The last thing he wanted was to have someone "fall over". A barbecue and one or two compulsory lunches – no excuses accepted – aided the bonding process.

Johnston's decision to opt for computer management of the case was driven purely by necessity. The time frame and the sheer extent of the inquiries required meant that it was the only answer. Like any other computer program, this one grew and grew. Initially it was just to be a matter of linking statements to photographs. Then exhibits were added, then the coronial material, a mapping system and, finally, all the video footage.

By the time the taskforce wound up in late August, the entire case was contained on a CD ROM. There were hundreds of statements, 1200 photographs, maps and diagrams, and a highly sophisticated cross-referencing system with coloured "flags" to highlight linkages.

The program permitted extraordinary detail. Something like the Broad Arrow Café could be presented as a basic outline showing the position of dead and wounded, with a zoom facility so detailed it could measure the distance between two taps on a handbasin. The positions of witnesses could also be featured, and it was possible to "navigate" around the entire case by clicking on a particular person or object. By clicking on a coloured dot on the outline of a witness, a summary of all evidence relating to that person could be obtained.

The "flags" within statements were other navigation points. A critical benefit to an investigation team is that constant cross-referencing during preparation will reveal any gaps in the investigations.

Individual printouts of specific material were a keystroke away. Access to the material was simply via a terminal, replacing the traditional cumbersome paper files, boxes of photographs and other exhibits. The taskforce also established a hard copy file.

On Friday, 16 August, the taskforce was wound up. Its investigation, and the development of the computerised case management, had taken just fifteen weeks.

The investigation had pieced together, bit by bit, the story of that terrible day. There was ample cause for satisfaction at police headquarters in Hobart, but this was tempered by the enormous impact that the Port Arthur massacre had had, not just on the Tasmanian community, but nation-wide.

The tragedy had begun when a strange and isolated young man named Martin Bryant woke in suburban New Town about 7 a.m. on Sunday, 28 April. Martin Bryant had packed a brightly coloured sports bag and placed it on the back seat of his Volvo. At 9.47 a.m. he had set the security alarm at 30 Clare Street and had driven off towards the Tasman Peninsula. By 10.30 a.m. he was at Midway Point, just past Hobart airport, where he stopped to buy a cigarette lighter at the local newsagency.

A person matching his description was then seen in nearby Sorell, 26 kilometres from Hobart, and then at Forcett on the road to Port Arthur, where he called in to a Shell service station and bought a cup of coffee, which he paid for with five and ten-cent pieces carried in a small tin, possibly a biscuit tin. Bryant had told the attendant that he was going surfing at Roaring Beach on the Tasman Peninsula because there were some "beautiful waves" coming down the beach. But Martin Bryant, with a surfboard on top of his car, had never surfed, and was known around the beaches of southern Tasmania as a "highway surfer".

Around 11.30 a.m. another motorist saw a vehicle fitting the description of Bryant's Volvo near Eaglehawk Neck, just 19 kilometres from Port Arthur. The driver matched Bryant's description, and he seemed to be thrashing from side to side as he drove. Half an hour later a similar car was seen to turn into the driveway of the Seascape guest house. Sally and David Martin, the owners of Seascape, were murdered not long after.

The police reconstruction of Bryant's strange journey turned up a bizarre encounter. A woman reported that her car had broken down on the highway just outside Seascape and that at about 12.30 p.m. another driver had stopped to give her assistance. She had been smoking a "joint" as she waited beside her car, and the good samaritan – who again matched Bryant's description – asked if there was anything for sale. She obliged with a fifty-dollar packet of cannabis. He told her to meet him at the Broad Arrow Café and shout him a cup of coffee for his help.

Martin Bryant had then driven 2.5 kilometres south along the Arthur Highway, past the historic site, and down the country road to Carnarvon Bay. He had called on Maurice and Jillian Williams, but they were not at home. He then stopped to talk to Roger Larner and mentioned that he might visit Marian Larner at the Larner house. Bryant then drove to Port Arthur and entered the grounds of the Port Arthur Historic Site.

With him he had a multi-coloured sports bag. In that seemingly innocuous sports bag Bryant had concealed a Colt AR15, with a magazine holding thirty bullets of .223 calibre. The gun was no more than a metre in length, and weighed, with the full magazine, less than 4 kilograms. A version of the M16 used by the American military, it has but one purpose – to kill or disable – and it does that very efficiently. In the boot of the Volvo, Bryant had two more weapons: a .308 calibre FN FAL fitted with a twenty-round magazine. It was a shade over a metre in length, and weighed less than 4 kilograms. There was also a twelve-gauge shotgun with a ten-round detachable box magazine. It was loaded.

The first to die in the Broad Arrow Café were two Malaysian tourists, Moh Yee William Ng, forty-eight, and Sou Leng Chung, thirty-two, from Kuala Lumpur. Then Bryant turned the gun on Mick Sargent, thirty, wounding him in the head before shooting dead Kate Scott, twenty-one. There was no chance of escape, it was all happening too quickly; and in any case, who could believe that a gunman was on the rampage in such a place? Later, survivors would recall that they had at first thought the sounds were of balloons popping, or perhaps that someone was banging on the roof.

Anthony Nightingale, forty-four, of Keysborough, Victoria, was the next victim, then Bryant took aim at a group of friends from Melbourne and Kilmore, Victoria. The range was point-blank, and within moments three of them – Kevin Sharp, sixty-nine, Walter Bennett, sixty-six, and Kevin's brother, Raymond, sixty-seven – were dead. Three others – Gary Broome, sixty-five, John Fidler, fifty-five, and Gaye Fidler, fifty-one – were wounded.

Martin Bryant was in control, total control, as he chose his targets. In all, twenty people died in the Broad Arrow Café and twelve were wounded. How long had it taken? No-one can be sure: it may have been as little as ninety seconds. Certainly it was no longer than two minutes, and in the first fifteen seconds, twelve people were shot dead. Then Bryant stepped outside the café and killed TigerLine bus driver Royce Thompson, fifty-nine, of Kingston, Tasmania, then Winifred Aplin, fifty-eight, of Banksia Park, South Australia. Janet Quin, fifty, of Bicheno, Tasmania, was shot down near one of the buses, and Elva Gaylard, forty-eight, of Hamlyn Heights, Victoria, died as she sheltered in a bus. Bryant at one stage went to the boot of his yellow Volvo for more ammunition and a change of weapon – the .308 FN FAL – as hundreds of visitors fled from the area, some running towards cottages or the ruins of the church, others to the motel on the hill, and some along the road back towards the toll booth. Incredibly, from the other side of the historic site, some tourists continued to walk towards the Broad Arrow, thinking that a re-enactment of some historical event was in progress.

Among those fleeing along the road towards the toll booth were Nanette Mikac, thirty-six, and her two children, Alannah, six, and Madeline, three. They were Martin Bryant's next victims – Nanette and Madeline shot dead as

Alannah tried to hide behind a tree just off the roadside. The terrified child was then shot dead from close range.

Bryant's rampage was not yet over, and he climbed back into the Volvo and accelerated towards the toll booth where other motorists, some of whom had seen the Mikacs shot, fled. Some were on foot. Bryant was seen to argue with Robert Salzmann, one of the occupants of a BMW parked beside the toll booth. Salzmann, fifty-eight, of Ocean Shores, had got out of the vehicle. He was shot dead. Russell Pollard, seventy-two, of Brunswick, New South Wales, was also out of the car and he too was shot by Bryant. The other two occupants, Robert Salzmann's wife, Helene, and Mary Nixon, of Crabtree, Tasmania, were killed where they sat and their bodies then dragged onto the roadway.

Bryant then transferred two of his guns, the Colt AR15 and the FN FAL, to the BMW, leaving the shotgun in the boot of his Volvo. Also left in the car, and later found by police, was his passport.

He drove off in the BMW, one of the guns protruding from the driver's side window, and skidded to a halt in front of the Port Arthur store and service station, a couple of hundred metres down the highway from the toll booth. He arrived as other motorists were giving a warning of what had happened at Port Arthur. They ran into the bush, or out through the back of the shop, as they saw the gunman approaching. Sydney couple Zoe Hall, twenty-eight, and Glenn Pears, thirty-five, were just about to leave in their car when Bryant leaped from the BMW brandishing a gun. Pears was ordered out of his car at gunpoint and forced to climb into the boot of the BMW. Bryant slammed the boot shut, then walked around to the driver's side of the car and shot dead Zoe Hall.

With his hostage trapped in the boot, Bryant drove 2.5 kilometres south along the Arthur Highway to the Seascape guest house, where he pulled up beside the road, stepped from the car, and took aim at approaching vehicles. It was just before 2 p.m. – less than half an hour since the first shots were fired at Port Arthur.

At least four cars were struck by bullets and four people were wounded – Canadian diplomat Simon Williams and his wife, Susan; Linda White, of Dandenong, Victoria; and Doug Horne, of Ferntree Gully, Victoria. Despite their wounds they managed to escape past Seascape to the Fox and Hounds Hotel about 800 metres further along the road towards Port Arthur, where they were assisted by hotel staff before the arrival of a Tasmanian Ambulance paramedic, James Giffard, and two volunteer ambulance officers, Jodie Branch and Roger Garth.

Bryant, meanwhile, had driven into Seascape, hauled Glenn Pears from the boot of the BMW and forced him into the house, where he handcuffed his hands behind his back, then used a second set of handcuffs to tether Pears to an immovable object. He then returned to the BMW, splashed petrol on it, and set it alight, as if to send a signal to police that here he was, and that he was waiting for them. The first police officer to see the blaze was Constable Paul Hyland, who had raced to the Port Arthur area from Saltwater River on the other side of the peninsula. The time was about 2 p.m. and the siege of Seascape was about to begin. Some time in the next few hours Glenn Pears would become the thirty-fifth victim of the Port Arthur massacre, but Bryant – identifying himself as "Jamie" – would claim that Pears and David and Sally Martin were still alive.

Only when he ran screaming from the house with his clothing in flames at 8.24 a.m. the next morning would the tragic truth be revealed.

Bryant was held in high security at Risdon gaol. He had made a brief return to hospital for skin grafts a few weeks following the massacre. The transfer had been cloaked in extraordinary secrecy: he was collected from the gaol at 6 a.m. by an ambulance. Before 10 a.m. he was back behind bars.

In the first weeks, a team of six officers maintained a 24-hour watch on him as he recovered from the severe burns received in the fire at Seascape.

The investigating taskforce had one major interview with him. It was conducted in a room at Risdon gaol in early July. The interview lasted about three hours, with a psychologist and a psychiatrist assisting police from outside the interview room. Throughout, Bryant was chatty, confident and occasionally cocky with his interviewers. At times he laughed and joked. A total of five police were involved, working in teams of two.

Bryant told them of his extensive overseas travels and of his liking for Austria and Switzerland. He made no admissions, and at one stage asked whether bail was possible. The interview was recorded on video. As the police were preparing to pack up, he told them he was sure they would find the person "who caused all this". With that, he pointed a finger into his chest.

"That's not very funny," one of the police officers commented.

Bryant replied that they should have put it on the recording.

"We are still recording at this present stage, so it is on the recording," the officer responded.

In that interview, Bryant told police that he had three guns and that over the previous five months he had bought a Daiwoo shotgun and a Colt AR15 from Terry Hill of the shop Guns and Ammo, in New Town, and that he had paid a total of $8000 in cash. Later he had bought a case (3000 rounds) of military style ammunition from Hill for $930. Bryant said he had never owned a gun licence and had not been asked for one.

It was not illegal, under Tasmania's then lax gun laws, to sell such weapons, but it was illegal to sell them to a person without a gun licence. Police confiscated about $80,000 worth of guns from Guns and Ammo on 2 November and said Hill's gun-dealer's licence had been revoked because of a failure to comply with requirements relating to gun dealers under firearms legislation.

Hill later denied ever selling guns to Martin Bryant, but said he had had some dealings with him, including an occasion when Bryant brought in an AR10 for repair. Hill said Bryant had produced a licence.

CHAPTER 24

As a Guest of Risdon Prison

Six months before Martin Bryant went to Port Arthur and killed thirty-five people, a group of tour guides from the historic penal site had made a visit to Risdon Prison, in Hobart, to compare the modern system with the one they tell the tourists about.

They had discovered some similarities, given that Port Arthur, for all its fearsome reputation, was regarded as enlightened for its time. There was an education system of sorts in place at Port Arthur, and probation was available. The greatest difference the guides found between the prison of early last century and today's institution was that prison officers today communicated much more with individual prisoners.

But Martin Bryant may well face a lifetime of virtual isolation in Risdon, given the risks that would be posed if he mingled with the general prison population. He spent the several months before his trial under tight security in a specially developed unit in the hospital section at Risdon. He had no access to the outside world, except through visits from his mother, Carleen, and his legal counsel. There were no newspapers permitted, and no television.

The unit was developed after an inquiry into Aboriginal deaths in custody, and involved a wall being knocked out to create a twin cell. The front is constructed of bulletproof glass, and the interior walls are largely made of stainless steel.

There are no suspension points, or sharp edges in the cell, and even the shower and the taps are controlled from outside. As a further measure, the cells on either side of him were left vacant, the one directly opposite was used as a storeroom, and he was kept under video surveillance.

Risdon, built in 1960, is the smallest of Australia's major prisons, with a capacity of 406, all in single cells. The present population is 267, and the prison is divided into four sections – maximum security, medium security, the women's prison and the prison hospital. There is also the minimum security Hayes prison farm beside the Derwent, north of New Norfolk.

Risdon has had its share of dramas in the past thirty years, with escapes and attempted escapes, and a strike by prisoners demanding an increase in their weekly living allowance.

It also has its own select band of "celebrities", including Mark "Chopper" Read, and Jack Newman, formerly Rory Jack Thompson. Thompson, who killed his wife in Hobart then chopped her body into small pieces and flushed it down the toilet, is held in the prison hospital.

The education program is regarded as one of the best in the country, and prisoners can enrol in a wide range of

TAFE and Adult Education courses, as well as general vocational training.

"Grant", a recently released prisoner who had served a couple of terms in what the locals call the "Pink Palace", said a normal day there was pretty good provided you had a job to occupy the time. Prisoners are employed in the laundry, bakery and kitchen, and some traineeships are available.

Like prisoners the world over, Martin Bryant will face the prisoners' code of ethics on the "inside", and the murder of the two Mikac children, Alannah and Madeline, will count heavily against him. "Grant" said that Bryant "would not last five minutes" with the other inmates. Those responsible for the deaths of children find themselves bracketed with paedophiles at the bottom of the pecking order.

The protection he will need will come at a high price for the Tasmanian community, already facing a bill for many millions as a result of the massacre. Ray Groom, the Tasmanian Attorney-General, has told state parliament that the cost of keeping Bryant in the gaol would be $200,000 a year, more than four times the state's average. "Obviously when you have a high security prisoner, it is a very expensive operation to make sure that the prisoner is fully secure," he said.

CHAPTER 25

The Trial of Martin Bryant

On 30 September, Martin Bryant was brought from Risdon prison to the Supreme Court in Hobart to answer seventy-two charges arising from the Port Arthur shootings: thirty-five counts of murder, twenty counts of attempted murder, three of causing grievous bodily harm, eight of wounding, four of aggravated assault, one of arson, and one of unlawfully setting fire to property.

The street outside the court was closed to traffic for three hours before the proceedings began. Sixty police, including the bomb squad and the Special Operations Group, mounted the biggest security operation in Tasmanian legal history. Unable to be accommodated in the court room, more than forty journalists covered the proceedings via a video link in an adjoining court room.

Martin Bryant pleaded not guilty to all charges in a hearing that lasted just twenty-three minutes. Witnessing the proceedings were a group of Port Arthur Historic Site workers, as well as friends and relatives of victims. Some wept or hid their face in their hands as Bryant answered the charges.

When the charge relating to Glenn Pears's death was read, the dead man's brother, Phillip Pears, shouted out in the court room: "You're a bloody coward, Bryant. Yours'll come soon!"

Pears was led away, and Bryant was remanded in custody by Chief Justice William Cox for trial at 10 a.m. on 19 November.

Soon after the hearing, Bryant and his defence counsel, David Gunston, parted company. Mr Gunston refused to make any public comment on the reasons or circumstances surrounding the decision, but there was speculation that he had expected his client to plead guilty.

Another senior Hobart barrister, John Avery, was approached to take over the defence. He visited Bryant in prison the following day, 1 October, and agreed to represent him. It was the first time John Avery had met Bryant face to face, but his wife remembered Bryant as the young man who came to their house selling vegetables years before.

The Tasmanian community then settled down to await 19 November and the beginning of a trial which could take up to a month. The Director of Public Prosecutions, Damian Bugg, with his staff, began contacting scores of witnesses around the nation. For many, particularly the people of the Tasman Peninsula, the prospect of a long and expensive trial in the lead-up to Christmas was cause for further stress and heartache.

Meanwhile, in Risdon prison, Martin Bryant continued his lonely and isolated existence, a routine broken only by visits from his lawyer and his mother. He had denied the charges, but the evidence against him was overwhelming.

Psychiatrists had dismissed suggestions that he was suffering from schizophrenia or some other major mental illness, so there was no defence on those grounds.

Shocked and deeply ashamed by what her son had done at Port Arthur, Carleen Bryant begged Bryant to tell the truth. She couldn't have faced the shame of going to court for a trial, so she told Bryant that everyone knew he was guilty and that he must tell the truth. But he refused. "They tell me I've done this and that," is all he would say.

A devout churchgoer, Carleen Bryant had almost had a nervous breakdown following the shootings and her son's arrest. The months since 28 April had been a living hell for her, and she spent some weeks in Western Australia with her daughter, Lindy, to escape media attention.

Back home, the front gate locked, Carleen Bryant was reluctant to venture outside, even to go to her local church on Sundays. She remained stunned by what Martin did. "The monster who did those things at Port Arthur was not my son," she said. "Martin was never violent, and I can't understand the guns. He had an air gun as a youngster, but Maurice smashed it after there were complaints that Martin was shooting out lights with it."

Carleen Bryant decided she would have to lie to her son to try to convince him to change his plea. She told him that if he didn't change his plea, she would commit suicide, and so would his sister, Lindy. He would never see them again, she said.

She had no idea whether her words had any effect. But gradually, in the weeks following his 30 September appearance in the Supreme Court, it seems that Martin Bryant came to accept that he should admit his guilt. Some three weeks after denying all seventy-two charges, while the rest of the community was preoccupied with the annual Royal Hobart Show on the other side of the river, he told his lawyer, John Avery, that he wished to change his plea.

On the afternoon of Wednesday, 30 October, the Tasmanian government issued a brief statement saying that Bryant would make a personal appearance at the Supreme Court on 7 November, twelve days before the scheduled trial date. The news took police and media by surprise, and immediately there were rumours that Bryant had decided to change his plea. The official word from the Director of Public Prosecutions was that it was a routine matter. "The prosecution and defence have sought an appointment for pre-trial discussions," Mr Bugg said. "This is a normal step in trials of this magnitude and was discussed with the Chief Justice at the last mention date. It is appropriate that these discussions should take place in the presence of Martin Bryant."

On 7 November, Bryant stood in the dock, wearing a light blue suit and an open-neck shirt. His counsel, John Avery, told Chief Justice Cox that, as this was Avery's first appearance before the court with his client, he thought it appropriate and instructive that the indictments be put again.

The judge agreed, and at 10.07 a.m. the first charge, that of murdering David Martin, owner of the Seascape guest house, was read to Bryant. "Guilty," Bryant replied quietly. Sixteen relatives of victims, as well as survivors of the massacre, were present in the gallery to hear him admit his guilt. Bryant repeated the word another seventy-one times over the next eighteen minutes. Occasionally he sniggered, smirked, giggled or smiled. It was a sad and bizarre performance which some onlookers, police among them, considered the result of stress, not amusement. It seemed that there was nothing callous about those laughs or sniggers. For all of his life Martin Bryant's responses had never fitted the norm; this was just another example. At one point, Mr Avery handed Bryant a glass of water, and later spoke to him about his conduct. Bryant nodded in response, and for a time was more composed.

Martin Bryant was remanded for a sentence hearing starting 19 November. Outside the court, Mr Avery refused to comment on his client's behaviour inside.

The Director of Public Prosecutions expressed relief on behalf of all those caught up in the massacre. "I'm relieved for their sake and for the community's sake," he said.

It is unlikely that it was Carleen Bryant's dramatic and tragic appeal that caused Martin Bryant eventually to admit that he had killed thirty-five people at Port Arthur. Instead, it may have been something much more mundane, such as a wish to get things over with, and his simple and misplaced belief that having done so, he could become a part of the general prison community, and perhaps have a television set in his cell.

One prison source spoke of Bryant's wish to "mix with the other guys". It seems that the strange young man who had never been able to look ahead and consider the results of his actions could not see that his life would always be endangered if he stepped into the prison yard with others.

Bryant was taken back to Risdon prison to await the final hearing. The following day, Tasmania's Tourism Minister, Ray Groom, announced that the Broad Arrow Café would be demolished before Christmas, and that work on a memorial at the site would start on 28 April 1997, the first anniversary of the shootings. A small part of the Broad Arrow, perhaps some steps and stone walls, would remain to give survivors and relatives of victims a focus for grieving and remembrance. The Minister said the memorial was likely to include a garden, a reflective pool, and a wooden cross bearing the names of the thirty-five people killed by Martin Bryant. In a grim footnote, Mr Groom said the demolition material would be taken to a secret location to thwart any attempt at ghoulish souvenirs.

On 19 November 1996 the sentencing hearing began in the Supreme Court, and Bryant, his hair cut short, listened as the full extent of his crimes was revealed by the prosecution, Occasionally he smiled, and sometimes even laughed.

In the court, Walter Mikac wept as he heard details of how his wife and two young daughters had been murdered. Walter Mikac would not be the only person to weep during the next two days, for in the court and surrounding rooms linked by video were 200 survivors, relatives and friends of victims, as well as members of the general public.

The Director of Public Prosecutions, Mr Damian Bugg, in completing his case on 20 November, read a victim impact statement compiled from the responses of 150 people who had described their pain. "There have been expressions of anger, sorrow, emotional and physical pain, a desire for retribution, despair in coping with the void caused by these crimes, and sense of hopelessness."

The emotional impact on the injured included feelings of loss of identity and depression. Sometimes suicidal tendencies were evident, he said. Families of the victims had described their lives as being totally destroyed. Mr Bugg ended his address by reading an excerpt from a letter written by a person who had lost loved ones at Port Arthur.

> I can but keep surviving to enshrine their spirit in the world. The incredible unconditional love, the warmth and freedom, the laughter, the dances, the spontaneity, cuddling and kissing, they are no longer there. I will, however, proudly endeavour to keep their spirits alive throughout my life. My love for them will never die and can never be taken.

Bryant's lawyer, John Avery, presented a 55-minute plea of mitigation in which he said that Bryant had been examined by two psychiatrists and a psychologist who had found Bryant was not mentally ill.

Professor Paul Mullin, a forensic psychiatrist from Melbourne, said Bryant initially gave the impression of being a normal young man. "It is only when you attempt to test his comprehension skills and numeracy that the extent of his intellectual limitation becomes clear," he said. "He functions in the borderline range between intellectual disability, and the dull, normal individual."

As a child Bryant had tortured and harassed animals, and he had tormented his younger sister too, said Professor Mullin. He appeared to have shown abnormalities in development from infancy and early childhood. "His physical, emotional and intellectual development was slow, he had considerable difficulties relating to other children, and his behaviour was often aggressive and disruptive."

Bryant had apparently told Professor Mullins that "All I wanted was for people to like me."

At the conclusion of the prosecution case, Bryant was asked if he had anything to say. He replied with just one word: "No."

As Martin Bryant was driven away in the prison van to begin his sentence, he left one question unanswered: why? Why would a childlike person, with a mental age of about twelve years, set out one day to murder so many people, the vast majority of them complete strangers, two of them young children? Why would such a man murder children, when he counted three other neighbourhood youngsters among his only friends and played happily with them for a year or so?

Martin Bryant conformed to no classic description of mental illness, and in his twenty-nine years he had no previous history of harming others. Indeed, he had walked out of a movie a few weeks before the shootings because he found the violence upsetting.

Police, psychiatrists and lawyers had all tried – and failed – to gain an adequate explanation from Bryant for what really lay behind his actions on that terrible Sunday. It may be that the truth in any real sense is beyond his capacity, and that any response he produces would be nothing more than fantasy or a form of words. He has shown no remorse, nor any sign that he realises the impact of what he did or of the community's feeling about his crime.

Awaiting sentence in his cell he laughed and joked and spoke of his past international travels – the travel he undertook in the desperate hope of meeting "normal people",

people who would respond to him, be his friend. He would attempt to strike up conversations with strangers he met overseas, only to be again rejected. In the end the things he enjoyed most were the long international flights, because these meant he could speak to people seated next to him. For them, unlike those in the street, there was nowhere to go. At other times in the prison before the sentence hearing it seemed he was most concerned about whether he would be allowed to have a television set in his cell. Occasionally he would say that he was worried that people on the outside might think him crazy. "I'm a bit eccentric," he cheerfully conceded in one conversation. There were times when he was almost likeable in a simple, superficial way. But he had always been so, as the customers on his vegetable round or the people who employed the strange young man to mow their lawns would attest.

Perhaps there were two flaws in the make-up of Martin Bryant which compounded to make 28 April 1996 – or something very similar – inevitable. First was the personality defect which prevented him from being able to connect with other people. Second was his inability ever to consider the consequences of things he did. Martin Bryant wanted friends. He wanted to be able to mix as other people mixed. But the socialising skills that most people develop, to greater or lesser degrees, were absent. He sent the wrong messages to his peers; he could not fit into group situations. He was isolated – increasingly so.

There were only two people with whom Martin Bryant felt secure: his father, Maurice, and the eccentric heiress Helen Harvey. Miss Harvey, Bryant told Professor Mullin, had been his only friend. Both died tragically within ten months of each other, leaving him without their stabilising influences. Martin Bryant was by then in his mid twenties, and more desperately alone than he had ever been. The money he had inherited gave him the freedom to indulge any whim, no matter what it cost, but it didn't buy him any real friends or respect. Bryant yearned to be noticed and admired, but nobody seemed to be listening, or to be capable of understanding what he was saying.

In the last few months before Port Arthur he came to the conclusion that his life was not worth living. Feeling lonely and rejected, he thought of suicide. For Martin Bryant there seemed to be but one alternative: he would have to do something to make people sit up and take notice. And Helen Harvey's money and Tasmania's lax gun laws meant he had the means to do it.

Fascinated by the gunplay in action videos, the young man spent thousands of dollars on military style weapons and ammunition at a Hobart gun shop. He then drove to Port Arthur, the place where he had spent much of his childhood, where he had been rejected by other children, where a family had refused his childish desire to buy their farm.

With thirty-five people dead, twenty others wounded, and a nation shattered by the horror of it all, Martin Bryant had achieved the recognition he had craved all his life. But he had not gained the respect. Instead, once more, he was shown to be what he had always been – a tragic and pathetic individual for whom society had no answers.

Chief Justice William Cox, in sentencing Martin Bryant on 22 November 1996, said it would be difficult to imagine a more chilling catalogue of crime. Bryant, grossly disturbed from early childhood and suffering from a severe personality disorder, had developed into a pathetic social misfit.

He sentenced Bryant to life imprisonment on each of the thirty-five charges of murder, and to twenty-one years imprisonment for each of the remaining thirty-seven charges. He ruled that Bryant not be eligible for parole.

Martin Bryant, the Port Arthur gunman, is in prison for the term of his natural life.

THOSE WHO DIED AT PORT ARTHUR, 28 APRIL 1996

....

Winifred Joyce Aplin, 58, Banksia Park, South Australia
Walter John Bennett, 66, Diamond Creek, Victoria
Nicole Louise Burgess, 17, Koonya, Tasmania
Sou Leng Chung, 32, Kuala Lumpur, Malaysia
Elva Rhonda Gaylard, 48, Hamlyn Heights, Victoria
Zoe Anne Hall, 28, Sylvania, New South Wales
Elizabeth Jayne Howard, 27, Eaglehawk Neck, Tasmania
Mervyn John Howard, 55, Dunnstown, Victoria
Mary Elizabeth Howard, 57, Dunnstown, Victoria
Ronald Noel Jary, 71, Redcliffs, Victoria
Tony Vadivelu Kistan, Summer Hill, New South Wales
Leslie Dennis Lever, 53, Redcliffs, Victoria
Sarah Kate Loughton, 15, Ferntree Gully, Victoria
David Martin, 72, Port Arthur, Tasmania
Noeline Joyce (Sally) Martin, 69, Port Arthur, Tasmania
Pauline Virjeana Masters, 49, West Ivanhoe, Victoria
Nanette Patricia Mikac, 36, Nubeena, Tasmania
Alannah Louise Mikac, 6, Nubeena, Tasmania
Madeline Grace Mikac, 3, Nubeena, Tasmania
Andrew Bruce Mills, 49, Mornington, Tasmania
Peter Brenton Nash, 32, Hoppers Crossing, Victoria
Gwenda Joan Neander, 67, Parafield Gardens,
South Australia
Mo Yee William Ng, 48, Kuala Lumpur, Malaysia
Anthony Nightingale, 44, Keysborough, Victoria
Mary Rose Nixon, 60, Crabtree, Tasmania
Glenn Roy Pears, 35, Neutral Bay, New South Wales

Russell James Pollard, 72, Brunswick, New South Wales
Janette Quin, 50, Bicheno, Tasmania
Helene Maria Salzmann, 50, Ocean Shores,
New South Wales
Robert Salzmann, 58, Ocean Shores, New South Wales
Kate Elizabeth Scott, 21, Balga, Western Australia
Kevin Vincent Sharp, 68, Kilmore, Victoria
Raymond John Sharp, 67, Kilmore, Victoria
Royce William Thompson, 59, Kingston Beach, Tasmania
Jason Bernard Winter, 29, New Town, Tasmania

HIGHWAY TO NOWHERE

RICHARD SHEARS

They were young, carefree and idealistic, the eight backpackers from Australia, Britain and Germany who, between 1989 and 1992, set out from Sydney to hitchhike south along the Hume Highway to Melbourne. Out on the highway their destinies became intertwined when they came face to face with evil. Seven were found dead, their mutilated bodies concealed in the beautiful eucalyptus forest south of Sydney.

Chillingly orchestrated, the slayings in the Belanglo State Forest shocked the world. To snare the highway prowler and bring him to justice would require total dedication and patience. Hundreds of police combed the forest for clues and sifted through mountains of information, studying forensic evidence and computer records.

Amongst the thousands of leads, one story stood out, of a young British backpacker's daring escape from a violent attacker. Paul Onions could give the police only the barest description, but it became a vital clue in the biggest man hunt in Australian criminal history.

Highway to Nowhere is unputdownable and unforgettable, the grisly but gripping tale of Australia's most terrifying and vicious serial killings.

ISBN: 0732251052

ENCOUNTER

KELLY CAHILL

Kelly Cahill was a young mother of three. She was also a sceptic — especially when it came to 'close encounters'. But driving home with her husband from a party late one evening along a lonely road in country Victoria, she was dazzled by a blinding light hovering above.

What happened next was at first too frightening to remember — until it became too terrifying to forget. As Kelly pieced together her memories of that fateful encounter, one detail stood out. There were other people there that night, people she didn't know or speak to. When researchers finally tracked them down, they're story was eerily similar.

Encounter is Kelly's story, her own, very personal account of an experience for which she has no rational explanation, an experience that has totally changed her life. Sometimes frightening, sometimes gut-wrenching and sometimes out of this world, it is a story that poses more questions than it answers. When you've read *Encounter* you'll discover, like Kelly, why a close encounter is impossible to forget.

ISBN: 0732257840